Safe Return Doubtful

Untold Stories of Greatness

Royal Explorers Club

~ Aldri Raadløs ~

REC Press
2015

A Royal Explorers Club Publication
© 2015 Royal Explorers Club
All rights reserved.

First edition: May 2015

Lazarus Royal
REC Press ed.
ISBN-13: 978-1507523216
ISBN-10: 1507523211

I. Lazarus	Editor / Typesetting
E. Lazarus	Curator / Master of puppets
K. Krohg-Sørensen	Illustration
A. Lazarus	Royal Guidance
M. Lazarus	Spiritual Inspiration
J. E. Lazarus	Security
G. Lazarus	Chartering
K. Lazara	Secretary / Liaison
K. Lazarus	Intelligence

REC Press,
Oslo, Norway
lazarusroyal@royalexplorersclub.com

Dedicated to the brave and sometimes plain stupid explorers and adventurers of forgone times.

"Never keep a line of retreat: it is a wretched invention."
\- Fridtjof Nansen.

CONTENTS

A part of man is not lead by reason. It acts with no regard to consequence. In the void between reason and madness painters become artists, travellers become explorers and men become legends. Do not fear death and what comes after, only a life without the prospect of living.

Will you take the road less travelled by?

Royal Explores Club, Spitsbergen 2015

PREFACE

*R*oyal Explorers Club is a small group of men unified in the hunt for adventure, armed only with guile, bravado and contempt for conventional wisdom. We draw our inspiration from the old explorers and adventurers of the world. The truly tough men of absurd principle, those who were often drawn to the ostentatious and grandiose. We find enjoyment in the stories of their tenacity, toughness and humour in the face of adversity.

Every chapter is inspired by real events, but the intention of this book is to excite and amuse the reader. Despite some creative liberties the stories ring true in spirit and in fact. The result is a collection of anecdotes that undoubtedly will both interest and impress the reader.

The Royal Explorers Club recognises extraordinary achievements and canonises those who brave the odds in the Royal Explorers Club's Annals of Honourable Persona. Each of the laureates have their own chapter in this compilation providing background for their nomination.

THE ESCAPE OF PETER FREUCHEN FROM THE BOWELS OF BAFFIN ISLAND

$\mathscr{P}$ETER Freuchen, one of the most astounding and celebrated arctic explorers, writers, anthropologists, journalists and travellers of Denmark, was born in Nykøbing Falster, Denmark in February of 1886. At a young age, he was known for his keen intelligence and thirst for knowledge and adventure. Even more, Freuchen grew into a hardy, burly man that shrugged off the assault of icy winds as though they were but mere snowflakes drifting onto his thick beard. Throughout his lifetime, he worked tirelessly, both in the field and behind the desk, to dispel the walls of ignorance surrounding the geography and culture of the far North. Moreover, as any resident or traveller of these beautiful yet oft barren lands can substantiate, extraordinary measures must at times be taken in the preservations of one's livelihood.

Notably, in 1910, Freuchen established the Thule Trading Station with a partner at Cape York, Greenland, the name Thule being chosen as it means to the far north, and the trading station being the farthest north base in the entire world. As such, this noteworthy location became the starting point for seven expeditions between 1912 and 1933, known as the Thule Expeditions. The first expedition was a spectacular journey of over 1,000 kilometres across inland ice that nearly killed man and dog alike, as Freuchen attempted to disprove the existence of a channel between Peary Land and Greenland, and in fact succeeded in such. Then president of the Royal Geographical Society, Clements Markham, called this journey the *"finest ever performed by dogs"*, which was indeed high praise, and marked the auspicious rise of Freuchen.

During his travels, Freuchen became quite engrossed with the Inuit culture, and in 1911 took a wife named Navarana; she followed him dutifully on several expeditions until her death by the Spanish flu. When Freuchen attempted to have her buried in the graveyard of a church, the church protested at her lack of baptismal status, and as such forbade the burial on their grounds. Distraught, Freuchen buried her himself. These actions separated Freuchen from the church and left him quite bitter towards them, and such feelings only intensified as he observed the dangerous and irresponsible actions of missionaries sent by the Christian church amongst the Inuit people. Christian doctrine presented a new world view to the Inuit, which often clashed with traditional beliefs and values. The missionaries neither understood nor cared to learn about the Inuit culture or traditions and discouraged many aspects of it - shamanism in particular.

Upon Freuchen's return to Denmark in the 1920s, he joined the Social Democrats as a writer and contributed numerous articles to the paper *Politiken*. However, this was not enough to scratch his itch for generating new and exciting ideas, and in 1932 Freuchen returned to Greenland on an expedition financed by the American Metro-Goldwyn-Mayer film-studios, and furthermore was employed by numerous film-studios as a scriptwriter and consultant, most typically to tap into his vast knowledge of Arctic cultures, geography and survival techniques. As Freuchen realised the contributions he had to offer, he founded The Adventurer's Club, a society for the compilation and celebration of discovering and understanding the mysteries of the world. Even today, this club exists and maintains its original, time-tested goals with distinction.

During the Second World War, Freuchen was devoutly anti-fascist, and as such worked incessantly with the Danish resistance movement against the Nazi regime, despite his loss of a leg due to frostbite in 1926, which had been replaced by a wooden leg. Freuchen became a high-priority target for the fascists owing to his linguistic ability and organisation skills, and was eventually captured due to overwhelming pressure on the movement as German troops gained a tighter hold on Denmark. He was imprisoned and sentenced to death by the fearful German authorities; afraid that even from prison Freuchen would inspire his fellow inmates to revolt and sabotage. Nonetheless, Freuchen remained resolute in the face of such bitter enemies. He was able to manipulate his escape, and from there fled to Sweden whilst continuing to outfox the Axis forces at every turn.

One of the strangest and most inventive, not to mention harrowing, circumstances of Freuchen's illustrious life occurred whilst exploring Baffin Island, which is located in the Canadian territory of Nunavut and holding the distinction of being the largest island in Canada and the fifth largest in the world. As Freuchen explored its frozen reaches, he found himself one particularly bitter day entombed in his very tent. Ice and snow coating its walls to such a degree that even

3

his great strength could not budge them. Using a bearskin from a bear he had killed and skinned himself earlier in the trek, Freuchen was able to create a small hole in the ice and hardened snow, but found an impassable barrier that blocked his progress, leaving the hole too small for his large, sturdy frame, as he found out attempting to climb through. In the attempt, his beard, coated in sweat and frost, became frozen to the runner of a sled. When he could not cut it free, he ripped his beard and flesh free with barely a grimace.

While thinking of some manner in which to escape this hellish predicament, Freuchen recalled his times at the helm of the dog sled. One particularly curious fact was how he observed the excrement of dogs that, left in the cold, became as hard and unyielding as a rock. Freuchen himself wrote in his memoirs *"Would not the cold have the same effect on human discharge?"* Desperate for some means in which to free himself, Freuchen saw no choice. *"Repulsive as the thought was, I decided to try an experiment."* Freuchen fashioned his faeces into a chisel-like instrument and, showing great forethought and patience, allowed for it to freeze through solid. He was delighted to find it functional. *"At last I decided to try my chisel, and it worked! Very gently and slowly, I worked on the hole..."* Within hours, Freuchen had freed himself from what might have been his own grave, and through his ingenuity, and strong stomach, prevailed against the fate ordained by the wilds. Thanks to Freuchen's innovative solution, cold weather survival guides and experts the world over now make sure to mention that, in extreme conditions, the utility of using one's "discharge" as a tool could mean the difference between life and death.

THE ANACHRONISTIC EXPLOITS OF "MAD" JACK CHURCHILL

$\mathcal{N}$ONE exemplify the ageless art of gentlemanly conflict more so than the British, and among their ranks, one man stands head, shoulders and waist above the rest: Lieutenant Colonel John Malcolm Thorpe Fleming Churchill. Churchill, oftentimes called "Fighting Jack Churchill" or, in the interest of brevity, "Mad Jack", was a British soldier that, armed with his iconic longbow, sword and bagpipes, acted with magnificent effect throughout World War II. With his motto of *"any officer who goes into action without his sword is improperly dressed,"* Mad Jack exuded the cultured, yet tempered, blood thirst of the career military man. Though his eccentric methods at times inspired dubious murmurings, his unabated effectiveness, both during wartime and peacetime, dissipated all objections.

Born in Surrey, a county in the South East of England, in 1906, Jack rapidly grew into a bright, determined young man. After receiving his education at King William's College on the Isle of Man, he went on to attend Royal Military Academy Sandhurst, which lies only a short distance south of London. Upon the completion of his training, during which time he showcased his archery and bagpipe ability for the 1924 film *The Thief of Bagdad*, Jack bid farewell to his native land to serve in Burma with the Manchester Regiment. There he would reside for a decade while honing his skills and bewildering the locals with his eccentric behaviour. In 1936, Jack briefly left the army to work as a newspaper editor, but the entity that is war could not allow one of its chosen to slip its bloody grasp. With the invasion of Poland by Nazi Germany and the Soviet Union in September of 1939, Churchill stowed his instruments of creation and took up once more his implements of destruction.

After resuming his commission with the Manchester Regiment, which had transferred from Burma due to the enemy action in Western Europe, Churchill began his auspicious journey through the Western theatre. In May of 1940, Mad Jack and his unit set upon a German patrol on the outskirts of L'Epinette, France from a point of surprise. Churchill ordered his men to await his signal, wherein he would strike down the first of the men with a loosed arrow from atop their tower. Mad Jack fired a single barbed arrow into his quarry, and the rest of the detachment rapidly fell by more conventional armaments. This remains the most recent recorded kill by bow and arrow in action, and Churchill is most certainly known for being the only British soldier to have felled a foe via this outdated yet still effective mode of death during World War II.

Shortly thereafter, Jack participated in the Battle of Dunkirk, which further emboldened his fighting spirit, and caused him to enlist with the British Commandos, where his volunteering was met with much agreement; Jack thought it sounded dangerous and exciting, and just the place for his sort. Mad Jack took part in Operation Archery, otherwise known as the Vaagso Raid, in an attempt to overthrow the entrenched German positions on Vågsøy, Norway on December 27th, 1941. Churchill, despite being appointed as second in command of No. 3 Commando, believed that men should lead from the front. Upon the ramps of the first landing craft falling onto the icy beaches of the stronghold, Churchill strode fearlessly into the chaos that war entails, heedlessly playing *The March of the Cameron Men* on his bagpipes, which disoriented and distressed the Germans while emboldening his compatriots. After a few protracted measures, Jack stowed his instrument and simultaneously primed and threw a grenade as he ran headlong into the battle in the bay. All the while expanding the British foothold due to sound direction and consistently high morale.

Thanks to the bombardment by Royal Navy gunships at dawn, fighters and bombers in possession of the Royal Air Force were able to mercilessly pound enemy strong points and weaken the tenacity of the defenders as the men on foot, Mad Jack chief among them, stormed the front, forcing the scattering Germans into a hasty, ill-planned retreat. The Nazi war machine used the area's fish-oil production and stores to aid in their manufacturing of high explosives, and it was the destruction of these targets, alongside important military installations in the area, that were the objectives of the ongoing operation.

Mad Jack and his men battled fiercely into the heart of Måløy, a town at the south end of the island, but encountered unexpectedly stiff resistance. A particularly elite unit of German troops belonging to the Gebirgsjäger, or mountain rangers, were on leave in Måløy, and upon the maritime

7

invasion came to the defence of the island. The mountain ranger's great proficiency in sniping and house-to-house combat slowed the British assault to a bitter slog of seizing the town street by street, building by building, in a perilous exercise of urban combat. British reserves were deployed to bolster the weakening offensive, and, much to the mirth of the British, a number of local citizens offered their aid by becoming porters for explosives and ammunition, as well as shepherding away the wounded and tending to them as best they could. By mid-afternoon, the town was in flames, and the various military stores, factories and installations had been destroyed.

As Mad Jack advanced through the town, he rampaged through a particular hut searching for military intelligence papers and similar useful articles. When opening a cupboard, he came across an undisturbed case of Moselle wine, which elated Jack to no end. However, at that exact moment, a demolition charge exploded in the near vicinity, knocking Jack to his back and leaving the hut a scattered pile of rubble. As Jack was carried away while cursing wildly in Scottish, due both to the nature of his non-lethal but painful injuries and his worry that the wine had been ruined, called out to his batman, or personal assistant, Stretton, to recover it for him. Later, wine in hand, he was furthermore assured that his bagpipes were still accounted for and fully functional. For his actions at Dunkirk and Vågsøy, Churchill was the recipient of the Military Cross and Bar, a prestigious honour meant for gallantry during active operations against the enemy.

By July of 1943, Jack, now a commanding officer with the British Commandos, led No. 2 Commando from their landing site at Catania in Sicily toward the town of Molina, where a German observation post controlled access to the city of Salerno through a narrow pass. Controlling the beachhead at Salerno was a major objective in Operation Avalanche, which was to occur in September of that same year. Still carrying his trademark Scottish longsword, bow and arrows, as well as his bagpipes, Jack struck a ludicrous yet imposing figure, and his men followed him without fail deep into enemy territory. Jack and a single corporal infiltrated the town while the rest of No. 2 Commando waited from a hidden vantage point. Dressed plainly, so as not to arouse suspicion, the pair wound their way through the town and, through the use of sheer bravado, intimidation and superior gunmanship, managed to capture the observation post. Jack and his corporal took forty-two prisoners, including a potentially deadly mortar squad, and led them down the pass while those wounded were carried on carts by their fellow German prisoners. Jack commented to a fellow commando that it was *"an image from the Napoleonic Wars."* Unsurprisingly, those higher in the chain of command were shocked at the brazen effectiveness of Mad Jack's actions, and awarded him the Distinguished Service Order, to further adorn his already overflowing chest.

After being knocked unconscious by grenades while playing *Will Ye No Come Back Again?* on his trademark bagpipes while attempting to seize the Croatian island of Vis, located in the Adriatic Sea, Jack was taken prisoner and flown to Berlin for interrogation in 1944. Unable to be broken, he was then shipped to the concentration camp of Sachsenhausen. From there, he and a fellow prisoner managed to escape through a drainpipe. They made for the Baltic coast by foot, where they were captured yet again, but only temporarily, as the war effort was going poorly, and the German war machine thought it best to see troops in active roles rather than guarding prisoners. After being released, Jack walked over 90 miles to Verona, Italy, where he met up with an American armoured force.

To Jack's dismay, the Atlantic theatre was at a close, so he hastened to Burma in an attempt to stem the Imperial tide in the Pacific, where the largest land battles against Japan were being fought. Alas, by the time Jack reached India, both Hiroshima and Nagasaki had been bombed, and peace had been enacted. Churchill was furious at this news, stating that *"If it wasn't for those damn Yanks, we could've kept the war going another ten years."*

THE PERILOUS DESCENT OF JEANNE-GENEVIÈVE GARNERIN IN THE "PARACHUTE"

$\mathcal{T}$HE consciousness of society is filled to the brim with men of fame and prosperity while the contributions of those women that push the boundaries of nature, shatter the beliefs of the multitudes or enlighten millions with discourse and discovery are frequently marginalised and held in disrepute. Such is not the case with Madame Jeanne-Geneviève Garnerin. Born in 1775 in France, she is known today as one of the earliest female balloonists and parachutists. She made great progress in both the alleviation of the moral stridency and the perceived contributions of women of the time, but these were hard-won battles, as is to be uncovered.

Jeanne was among the fevered crowd at Parc Monceau watching André-Jacques Garnerin, later to be appointed Official Aeronaut of France for his actions, as he prepared for his very first hydrogen balloon flight and parachute descent on October 22th, 1797. So enthralled was she with this fantastic and otherworldly endeavour, as indeed his rise from the earth and eventual return was done with aplomb and rather exceptional poise, that she hastened to make his acquaintance, and indeed she was greeted rather favourably. Enchanted by her manner, ambition and grace, André took to this without hesitation. In the coming months, they grew into a pupil and mentor relationship, and as Jeanne's knowledge grew, her desire to ascend to the sky like the Gods of old grew as well. As the nature of André's work came further into the forefront of the public eye, suspicions were raised and doubts were cast upon the moral fortitude of his work and methods.

In 1798, as weather improved and the visions of once again mounting the world loomed forever clearer in the mind's eye, André made his stunning proclamation: he was to take a woman, Citoyenne Henri, up with him for his next ascent. This cause célèbre resulted in a stir in France that was scarcely witnessed on such a scale. Although the public and the press were decidedly in favour of this voyage into the air, André was called to appear before the officials of the Central Bureau of Police, as they had severe doubts as to the validity of such an endeavour. Their concerns were twofold: firstly, they had reason to believe that the vast changes in air pressure could wreak absolute havoc on the delicate organs of the female body, which was widely considered to be fragile and prone to failure by the medical community. Furthermore, they put forth the idea that a man and a woman in such close proximity and privacy was to prove to be a temptation beyond the ability of any human to resist.

When questioned about these concerns, André responded that he expected nothing untoward to occur and he accepted personal responsibility for any mishaps that could potentially occur during the flight. However, the Bureau remained unsatisfied by such lofty proclamations, and, believing themselves to be a moral as well as legal police, issued an injunction against André forbidding him from going forth with the event as planned. The injunction stated that the young woman, foolish and meek as she was, knew not what she was committing herself to, and thus needed to be protected from her own dangerous whims.

Refusing to accept this abomination of a ruling, André appealed to the administration of the department with haste. After heated consultations with the Minister of the Interior and Minister of Police, the injunction, and injustice, was overturned. A statement concerning the incident was released to the press, indicating that this was based on the grounds that *"there was no more scandal in seeing two people of different sexes ascend in a balloon than it is to see them jump into a carriage."* Furthermore, they were impressed at the sheer moxie of a woman's drive to be part of this historic event. And indeed, the flight went flawlessly.

Following Citoyennes success, Jeanne too went up with André on November 10th, 1798, and this brief taste of freedom stoked the fires of audacity. Afterwards, her ambition towards a solo flight and the desire for being the first woman to jump from a balloon with a "parachute" were triggered. This desire to attain such singular heights was never put in ink, but it seemed to stem from the oppressive social environment that ladies of all social statuses were subjected to. Disregarding etiquette and the well-mannered conduct expected from her, she devoted all her time to her newfound goal and toiled tirelessly to aid in perfecting the "parachute."

Years after her solo flight, on October 11th, 1802, she would submit this patent application, going into grave detail on the design and construction, far beyond this excerpt:

"... [for] a device called a parachute, intended to slow the fall of the basket after the balloon bursts. Its vital organs are a

cap of cloth supporting the basket and a circle of wood beneath and outside of the parachute and used to hold it open while climbing: it must perform its task at the moment of separation from the balloon, by maintaining a column of air."

On October 12th, 1799, the culmination of Jeanne's struggles came to a head. As hundreds gathered at Parc Monceau, crowding its English-style curved walkways and informal layout. Curious residents and tourists alike admired the endearing follies before transitioning to the state of the onlooker, chattering with trepidation as the imposing balloon was fitted for take-off. Its "parachute" still very much a prototype, with a reliability that would have merited grave failings by today's standards. After making certain that weather conditions were perfect for the event, Jeanne stepped onto the undercarriage alone. Her many friends cheering her onwards and giving her the renewed willpower to cross both physical and societal horizons. As the anxious crowd gathered for the departure, lines were cut and weights cast off, and gently the balloon bobbed into the sky, no longer tethered to the safety of land.

Higher and higher Jeanne soared, and the landscape of Paris dwindled to little more than a multi-coloured patchwork by the reckoning of the naked eye, groves smudged into browns and greens, oranges and yellows, reds and blacks, a veritable autumnal blooming intermingling with the stark stone, brick and cured wood of the more developed districts. Plains spilled forth, boasting their harvest-time crops while pastures in disorganised jumbles dotted here and there. Jeanne absorbed it all, rising higher than ever before, seeing what neither man nor woman had seen in full sight with such clarity.

Yet, keeping track of her progress in great detail, and careful not to become so enraptured by the scene as to endanger herself more so than already by mere virtue of this ascent, Jeanne recognised that the time to cut away had come. Having risen to the worrisome height of 900 meters, she had thrust her fate into the province of careful planning and calculation. With one last wistful view towards the ever dominating Heavens, and making sure she was quite secure within the basket, Jeanne cut away her lifeline, allowing no time for hesitation. Free fall! A moment's suspension in nothingness, and the briefest inkling that the worst had happened, for there were no methods of recourse. Indeed, this day fortune favoured the prepared, and with a monumental unfurling and lurch, the "parachute" extended in its entirety, slowing the descent to a pleasant, easily endured drop towards the ground. Despite having no way to steer, Jeanne was blessed yet again by a safe landing after many long minutes. She was soon met by astounded onlookers and congratulatory welcomes back to Earth. This barrier broken, she went on to complete many more ascents and parachute drops across France and Europe abroad, and in doing so ignited the passions for women's liberation and aeronautical exploration alike.

Capt. James Cook and his Ascent to Godhood amongst the Islanders of Hawaii

HROUGHOUT known history, there are few adventurers held in such imposable esteem as that of Captain James Cook. Navigator, cartographer, explorer - these are but a few of the titles bestowed upon a Captain of the Royal Navy and fellow of The Royal Society of London for Improving Natural Knowledge. Born on November 7th, 1728, Cook joined the British Merchant Navy as a teenager, where his quick grasp of seamanship and a keen eye for detail led to his induction into the Royal Navy in 1755. After his participation in the Seven Years' War, during which time he partook in the surveying of the Saint Lawrence River during the Siege of Quebec, he was brought to the attention of the Admiralty and Royal Society as a man of prodigious worth and ability. This in turn led to his commission in 1766 as commander of *HM Bark Endeavour* for the first of three Pacific voyages.

In these embarkings, Capt. Cook traversed thousands of miles of barely understood and even unknown waters, from New Zealand to Hawaii, describing them in such cunning and complex detail as had never been accomplished until his keen eyes spied the landmarks and his adroit fingers marked them so exactly. Through uncountable occasions of difficult, even deadly, conditions, Cook displayed his worth time and time again by means of superior ability in all matters related to sailing, cartography, leadership and perseverance through the harshest of seas. His eventual death was a terrible loss to the scientific community, but he left behind a legacy of geographical knowledge, which served as a great influence to his numerous successors even into the twenty-first century. The circumstances of his death, however, are worthy of a recount, for such an extraordinary series of events have not again been seen to this very day.

The *HMS Resolution*, which Cook was the newest commander of, was off the coast of Hawaii in the winter of 1778, the vessel being described as *"trees moving about on the sea"* by one of the rather confused natives. Upon Cook's approach at Hawaii Island, the largest of the archipelago, he made landfall at Kealakekua Bay on January 16th, 1779. By chance, his arrival coincided with Makahiki, a Hawaiian harvest festival of worship of the Polynesian god Lono. He encountered thousands of Hawaiians in canoes, each of them brandishing lavish items of great worth in an obsequious manner, in particular a feathered cloak constructed from rare tropical birds and a handsome helmet of outstanding native craftsmanship, both presented to Cook. Although a bit ruffled at the unkempt appearance of the natives, their warm welcome put the crew of the *Resolution* at ease, and they proceeded with cautious, reserved interaction with the overly generous gift bearers. In discussions taking place, it was uncovered by Cook that these savages were not this welcoming for no reason; they seemed to believe that the festival coinciding with the arrival of the *Resolution*, which bore masts and rigging that provided similarities between it and the trappings of Lono, meant the arrival of Lono!

Capt. James Cook was intrigued by this mistaking of deific significance on his part, as the natives considered Cook to be the sex god Lono incarnate. His worship, including the presentation of countless fertile, nubile women for his taking, proved to be a powerful tempter, and Cook decided to embrace the islanders as they had embraced him. Cook was treated as a deity that walks amongst mortals, with such pampering and subservience as befitting a man of such an imposed status.

Its participants adorned with flower necklaces and pig fat, the festival evolved into an orgy of lecherous action, punctuated by fireworks that had been stored on the *Resolution*. After a month's stay, during which time Cook sampled countless willing women, he was forced to press onwards, as even the offer of a life filled with endless pleasures and ease was not enough to stay the desires for knowledge and science bursting from within his chest. After a tearful ceremony, the *Resolution* departed with Cook and his crew on board, oblivious to his imminent violent end.

Shortly after the departure, the foremast of the *Resolution* broke beyond repair, and Cook was forced to return to Kealakekua Bay with the intention to anchor there. However, his return was after the season of Lono, which resulted in a series of quarrels between the natives and the Europeans. On the 14th of February 1779, it was recorded that a boat belonging to the *Resolution* was lost to the pillaging, nefarious hands of some of the islanders. As was the traditional response to such ill deeds, Cook and his men attempted to take hostage of the King of Hawaii, Kalani'ōpu'u-a-Kaiamamao, also called Tereeboo, King of Owhyhee, with the intention of returning

19

the king upon the return of the stolen boat. Capt. Cook took to the beach with a number of marines at his side, armed, armoured and trained, and attempted to abscond with the royal member. Despite the fierce assault and heavy losses at the well-equipped hands of Cook and his men, the sheer number of disciplined and hardy natives drove the crew back to the shorefront. The meagre foothold that was briefly established was swallowed whole by the surf and the proud people of the island, and slowly, inevitably, the tide shifted, and what had at first been deemed a rout became a ferocious counterattack that broke the will of the sailors.

Cook, a father and leader to his men, as always, attempted to reorganise and make a tactical retreat with his remaining marines and began to help cast their boats off and back into the deeper waters. As he did this, he was struck from behind on the head, and sank to his knees in the surf, dazed and dying, as he saw his men off to safety. Cook was then set upon with knives and spears and run through many times as the ocean water darkened with his blood. Nonetheless, he was still held as a worthy man in the eyes of the islanders, and his body underwent funerary rites befitting the highest regarded elders. The corpse was disembowelled and baked, the flesh falling from Cook's bones in charred clumps. The bones that were left were preserved, some of which were gifted to the Europeans after they demanded his return, thus allowing Cook a proper burial at sea, as befitting a man of his stature and high rank. Cook left the world as he had entered it: bathed in blood amidst the screams of those seeking his presence and abhorring it all the same.

The Life and Accidental Death of John Kendrick at the Receiving End of Friendly Grapeshot in the Waters off Fair Haven

*J*OHN Kendrick was born in the infancy of colonised America in the year 1740, when the British Crown was still delving deep into the woodlands, plains and mountains of unspoiled beauty to pilfer its resources to fuel their empire. Raised in a small coastal town in Massachusets in a seafaring family, John wanted to become a sea captain. Like many of John Kendrick's time and station, he received but a simple education, but this did not impact his sharp wit and keen eye for business. At the age of 20, he joined a whaling crew where a burgeoning familiarity with the grapeshot used as cannon ammunition would be no soothing balm in his time of reckoning. This was hazardous work indeed, but it toughened John to the life of the seaman, and in 1762, he participated in the French and Indian War to some minor acclaim. At war's end, he built up his fortune in business and became the owner of several merchant ships over the course of the next decade, but the truly inspiring tales of his life only began at the advent of revolution.

Throughout his life, Kendrick had a deep and abiding love for his country and his countrymen. Upon feeling the rumblings of the long-awaited uprising, Kendrick was eager to throw in his lot. He was shored during the Boston Tea Party of 1773, and personally threw in several crates of the distasteful leaves while taking deep draughts from an American brewed lager that was always nigh-full due to the many flowing barrels provided to the thirsty patriots. Kendrick's blood boiled at the mere thought of breaking Britain's iron grip on the fledgling lands, and went on to serve as commander of the privateer *Fanny*. This proved to be an auspicious turning point for the now near middle-aged Kendrick, as the *Fanny* then went on to be the very first ship in the new Continental Navy during the American Revolution.

The *Fanny* was a large, powerful vessel of some 18 guns and about 100 crewmen, and she, with Kendrick at the helm, seized several ships from the English throughout the war. These successes proved to be of an extraordinary value, due to the acquisition of money and supplies from the captures, as they gave a much-needed boost to the American war machine. In fact, several ships contributed partially to the building of Kendrick's home in Wareham, Massachusetts. However, even the experienced Kendrick at the helm was unable to avoid his ship's capture by overwhelming British numbers, and he was taken prisoner in November of 1779. The Continental Navy, realising the value of Kendrick due to his devout service and fame, had him released via a prisoner exchange. Now a free man, Kendrick took command of the brigantine *Count d'Estang* and its sixteen guns and hundred-plus crewmen. He even commanded another brigantine, the *Marianne*, later that year, and went on to serve admirably and with great distinction until war's end in 1783, at which time he returned to whaling and coastal shipping until the young republic rallied men for the first American ships of discovery.

In 1787, Kendrick became commander of the *Columbia Rediviva*, alongside the sloop *Lady Washington*, upon the embarking of the so-called Columbia Expedition, which was financed by a wealthy syndicate led by a Boston merchant by the name of Joseph Barrell. After leaving the ports of Boston harbour on October 1st, 1787, the two ships found themselves at Cape Verde Islands on November 9th, and then Brett's Harbour on the western side of the Falkland Islands February 16th, 1788. These stops were but brief interludes on Kendrick's dash, and on the 28th, Kendrick pressed onwards, despite being urged to wait the rest of the winter in the Atlantic waters. Thus, Kendrick rounded Cape Horn and deviated from his path southwest into the Antarctic waters, instead heading northwest into the Pacific. As the *Columbia Rediviva* and *Lady Washington* rounded the tip, they lost sight of one another in a horrid wintry storm and were unable to re-join for the remainder of the journey.

Kendrick, weathering the storm with nigh his cloak askew, continued forth to the Juan Fernández Islands with, much to his chagrin, two men dead and several sick with scurvy, while he of hardiest constitution remained unphased. The buoyant vessel pressed onwards, reaching Friendly Cove in Nootka Sound without further incident, where the *Lady Washington* was fortunately docked. At Nootka Sound, Kendrick decided to stay and befriend the native Nuu-chah-nulth people, for, unusual people though they were, it would give the Americans a solid edge in fur trading in the area, as two British vessels had been spotted at Nootka Sound upon Kendrick's arrival. After several months in building up the relationship between himself and the natives, Kendrick left with the advantage in the fur trade, and utilised it to great effect in the coming years.

At the end of June, Kendrick came to Vancouver Island and traded with the Haida people on the Queen Charlotte Islands, but was deeply embittered with them due to their heinous secretive theft of a great deal of the crew's clothing. A crime which Kendrick remedied by locking their chief, Coyah, to the base of a cannon and threatening to push it into the sea unless the clothing was returned, which was done so with great expediency. Kendrick, in his great capacity for forgiveness, returned to the island two years later in an attempt to begin trading once more, but the Haida, in what was later found to be a grave error, attempted an attack on the crew. Despite the early loss of a chest of arms to the attackers, Kendrick and his officers fought off the incursion, even when Coyah non-fatally cut Kendrick's abdomen. So enraged was Kendrick by this assault that he executed a native woman that had encouraged the attack while she floundered in the waters, as well as exterminated numerous others with small arms and cannon fire as they fled Kendrick's awe-inspiring wrath. Coyah himself was forced to abandon his tribe in disgrace.

On December 3rd, 1794, Kendrick, now captain of the *Lady Washington* arrived at Honolulu, Hawaii - which was at the time called Fair Haven - to find a pair of English vessels aiding in the defence of some as-yet-acquainted natives against some other nameless ones. Kendrick threw in his lot with the English, as he found this advantageous to the potential for future trade. The battle itself is unimportant, for an occurrence of such unfathomable rarity occurred that next morning, which left all those that bore witness in such a state of shock as to leave them questioning their very faith.

At 10 o'clock of December 12th, 1794, the mid-morning bringing with it a cooling breeze and moderate chop to the foamy waters, Kendrick's brig fired a thirteen-gun salute to which the *Jackal*, which bore the English upon its deck, answered with its own salute. However, the incompetent, unobservant British sailors made a hasty, easily found error. Instead of loading their cannons without ammunition, they left one of their cannons loaded with a hefty amount of grapeshot. Tragically, the grapeshot smashed into the side of the *Lady Washington*, leaving gaping holes in its hull and wreaking havoc amongst the crew. Much to the shock of everyone on board, several balls of lead flew through Kendrick's table on deck, where he sat with some of his men. Their bodies were torn apart by the freak accident, and sorrowfully Kendrick and his men were taken ashore. Behind a secret grove of palm trees, they were buried solemnly in the beach sand. The crew of the *Jackal*, filled with horror by their oversight, dug with bare hands and bare backs in an act of contrition and to incur a minor measure of forgiveness for the wrongs they had committed.

THE ECCENTRIC LUSTS OF
BENJAMIN HORNIGOLD

*I*n the early eighteenth century, the numerous cays, islets and islands of the Atlantic Ocean, southeast of the North American mainland, were ripe for exploitation and plunder, and one of the earliest of such infamy was Benjamin Hornigold. Born of inauspicious beginnings, probably in the late seventeenth century near Norfolk, England, he likely began to serve on ships out of King's Lynn or Great Yarmouth, seaside towns on the eastern coast of England. Little to nothing is known of his familial relations or aspirations of the time, but for whatever reason, Hornigold was drawn to the New World, and it was there he observed the golden goose eggs floating haplessly amongst the Bahamas. Hornigold, possessing a clever mind and quick wit, decided to seize the opportunities so generously presented to him. His early life of frequent want of basic needs was rapidly discarded in favour of frivolous desires and idle musings; he became the sort of dangerous man with whom one placated rather than challenged, no matter the curious fire that seized him.

Hornigold's first recorded acts of piracy took place in the winter of 1713 and 1714. Shortly after his arrival in the Bahamas, he managed to obtain several sailing canoes, otherwise known as periaguas by the local natives, and a small yet formidable sloop, a one-masted vessel with a minor armament of cannons. Taking on a crew promised riches if following under his command, Hornigold menaced the plethora of merchant ships arriving and departing off the coast of New Providence, one of the largest and most populated islands of the Bahamas. Utilising his excellent seamanship and careful choice of targets, Hornigold was widely successful and was able to rapidly increase his wealth and fearsome reputation throughout the region.

By the year 1717, Hornigold had managed to increase his fleet through several forced acquisitions, amongst them a massive thirty-gun sloop named the *Ranger*, almost certainly the most powerful vessel throughout those waters at the time. Hornigold grew bolder through the years, and with the *Ranger* as his flagship, he was able to seize almost any vessel with nigh impunity, such was the strength he brought to bear. During this period, Hornigold's second-in-command was Edward Teach, a man of great loyalty and surpassing ferocity. Teach was far better known in later years as Blackbeard, the terror of the Atlantic waters. The duo was legitimately unassailable at the peak of their maritime strength.

In the beginning of 1717, the two pirate captains managed to forcefully take three merchant ships in quick succession. The ships carried loads of flour, spirits and white wine respectively. This brazen assault incited the rage of the Governor of South Carolina, leading to a merchant ship being heavily armed and sent out to subdue and perhaps even capture the *Ranger* and her supporting vessels. In March of the same year, the *Ranger* assaulted the merchant ship, easily overpowering it and forcing it aground on Cat Cay, leaving the Governor's expedition an unmitigated failure. The captain of the shamed ship scarcely made it back to report alive. A member of the captured ship described the fearsome scene: Hornigold's fleet had increased to five sizable ships, crewed and manned by easily over 350 pirates, sailors, stewards and men-at-arms. He had become the most domineering figure within a thousand square miles, and whatever vessel sailed in his view, he could take by force.

During the heated summer of 1717, Hornigold opted to sail off the coast of the Honduras, to prey on the numerous ships coming to and fro to deliver the raw materials and manufactured goods that oiled the gears of the British Empire. Spirits were high amongst the men, and Hornigold's fleet was, as always, greatly successful, even when meagre defences were mounted against his overwhelming forces. They feasted nightly on succulent meats and heady spirits while their ships became festooned with memoirs of their takings. Despite the festivities, the fleet remained immensely formidable, and none was able to demand upon them. After one evening of particularly intense merriment, wherein many of the men lost their hats in the excitement, the fleet happened upon a sloop that was primarily in current use as a method of passage for a number of people of the higher class, and indeed were they dressed rather fashionable despite the oppressive humidity and heat. Their coverings, in particular, were ostentatious to the point of absurdity, with great feathers and wild colours in abundance.

Almost lazily, the fleet pulled up alongside the sloop, which surrendered immediately, naturally, as the fleet was well known and feared by all in the area. The *Ranger* extended its boarding armaments across and allowed the crew, Hornigold amongst them, to stumble across, all of them inebriated still from the continued celebrations due to their many successes. As the crew of the subdued sloop obediently arranged themselves on its deck, their splendour in full adornment, Hornigold squinted in the noonday sun, a half-empty bottle of rum in his hand, and appraised his newest acquisition. He sweltered in the scorching temperatures, with no reprieve for his uncovered head. Most of his crew were similarly unshaded.

Hornigold spied on the numerous hats of various styles, shapes and sizes, indicating the status of their wearers. Almost solemnly, and indeed with grave seriousness, he slurred his way through an explanation for this delay, speaking of how in a fit of madness many hats were thrown overboard into the choppy waters the previous night. The group listened with trepidation and curiosity at the odd speech, both fearing for their lives and utterly confused by the display. At Hornigold's conclusion, he strode up to a likely gentleman and snatched the hat right off his head, to which the startled man stood still in shock. Following their captain's example, the rest of his crew did the same, taking their picks as they saw fit. Now refitted with a wide-brimmed, shady head covering, Hornigold gave an awkward bow, thanking the hostages for their contribution. With a final swig, he tossed his bottle aside, which exploded in a shower of glass and droplets on the forecastle, and wandered his way back aboard the *Ranger*, his wide-eyed men in tow. As the fleet sailed away, the sweating men of the freed ship were both incredulous and thankful for their lives, as they had been spared by the desire, not for spices, spirits and silks, but merely for relief from the blazing sun above.

THE MOUNTAIN MAN OF
GEHLAUR, INDIA

$\mathcal{D}$ISTINCTION needs not come from travelling the world and taking in its wonders, nor from impacting millions with far-flung goals and unshakable charisma. A man's reputation is only as good as his deeds, and those deeds can be minor or herculean in nature - but what truly sets one apart from the crowd is the drive, determination and focus to achieve, despite whatever obstacles that may present themselves. Ridicule from the ignorant and disbelieving must be left behind, for greatness can not be burdened by such. Dashrath Manjhi took these beliefs as truths when he began what is today one of the most monumental tasks ever undertaken by a single man.

Manjhi was born into a poor labouring family in Gehlaur village a few miles outside of the city of Gaya in North-Eastern India in 1934. He had settled for a simple life as his forefathers had before him, and spent his days toiling in the fields several kilometres from the village. In between lay a number of treacherous, crumbling hills, with only a narrow footpath winding through them for transit, so dangerous that it disallowed all vehicles and required several hours of hiking. These hills isolated Gehlaur from the rest of the region and were a frequent source of pain for the community. Numerous petitions to the Indian government for a proper road to be built were ignored or idly swept aside, as few officials cared about the problems of the backwoods workers that offered little in the way of taxes or political support. And so, men, women and children travelled the broken path daily to reach their cultivations and school, and back again come nightfall.

Manjhi was well aware of the ills of this geological landmark, knowing that it had troubled his village for centuries, and likely would continue to do so. Intervention by anyone seemed unlikely, so Manjhi steeled his resolve and decided to take upon himself this task: to build a 360 foot long, 30 foot wide path, to be cut right through the craggy rock of the hills, at times up to a depth of 25 feet. He began his arduous task in 1960 with nothing but a chisel, hammer, shovel and his back. The spark of inspiration came from his wife, whom he cared for deeply. While he worked, unshaded from the blazing sun above, his wife sought to bring him water to relieve his parched throat. She attempted to carry it over the hills, using the ancient footpath worn into the rock, but slipped on the uneven ground, and was wounded terribly. The day of the accident was the day Manjhi decided to undertake this seemingly impossible mission.

Dashrath Manjhi was immediately met with laughter and scorn by the very people he was trying to help. Idiot, fool, ignorant - these are but some of the labels so harshly given to him as he was passed by day after day as he slowly whittled away at the unyielding rock. None, except his dearly beloved wife, thought it could be possible to overcome this barrier with nothing but the strength of one's arms, and so mockery was the order of the day. Such cruelty Manjhi faced, from the very people he intended to aid, did not bend his will; truly, his work redoubled in spite of such opposition.

Dashrath's wife gave him the initial motivation to take up his tools and conquer the unassailable. She also gave him the fuel of love and support to see his task through. However, not long after taking up his tools, his wife became ill and rapidly sickened, passing away after a brief interlude. Despite her quick deterioration, she remained hopeful and supportive of her husband, even to her deathbed. Manjhi vowed to see the project through to the last stone, in her honour.

His spirit renewed, Manjhi worked at the mountainous pass like a man possessed, day and night, with nary a moment to eat or sleep. His desire to see his work completed assuaged all doubts and fears, and, as the years passed and his work continued unabated, the villagers came to realise that Manjhi could not be broken. The taunts and murmurs began to cease, and a quiet optimism took hold of the village of Gehlaur as the years took their toll both on the rock beneath Manjhi's feet as well as his body. Help took the place of ridicule, and a sparse few offered words of encouragement, as well as more concrete aid, such as food or tools. Dashrath was humble and accepting of anything that was offered to him, but wished to single-handedly carve through this massive hill, and so his self-ordained task was continued alone.

Although the considerations of his fellow man had been swayed by the relentless ferocity of Manjhi, nature itself would not be assuaged by such devotion. Wind and storm besieged the rock with uncaring force while the harsh sun beat down in their shadows absence. Yet Manjhi tirelessly continued to cart away load after load of rubble, and as over two decades passed him by, his trial came closer and closer to fruition.

Finally, in 1982, Dashrath completed his task: a road carved by a single man, alone but for the eventual support of his community and the everlasting love of his wife. One hundred and ten meters in length, nine meters wide and up to seven and a half meters deep into the hills. This testament to the endurance of man caused what was once a perilous, arduous hike across the broken ground of the Gehlaur hills to be a straightforward, relaxing walk that even the least surefooted of the locals could manage with ease.

Manjhi was celebrated locally for his enormous feat, and over time gained national acclaim for his accomplishment of the seemingly impossible. However, there was never any recognition from the government of India concerning his contribution, but this did not dissuade Manjhi from basking in the joys of his labour. Day and night, he hewed the earth to make the lives of the people he cared for safer, and over the course of twenty-two years, he finished his life's work. His fulfilment came not from the impassive stance of his government, nor the adoration of his people, but from completing his promise to his long-deceased wife, and from making certain that the fate that had befallen her need not occur again.

Manjhi lived out the rest of his life revered and honoured by the community of Gehlaur village and was quite content to enjoy the fruits of his work and rest his weary bones. Up until his death in August of 2007, he was sought out as a source of wisdom, a symbol of the ability man can harness if only they had the willpower to do so. Manjhi may never have journeyed the oceans, wrestled ferocious beasts or ruled a nation, but he offered himself in generosity and humility to serve humanity, and for that, he is remembered.

The Exploits of Dr. Livingstone in the Heart of the Wild Continent

$\mathcal{O}$NE of the greatest and most influential national heroes of Great Britain and her colonies, Dr. David Livingstone - pioneer, missionary, explorer - devoted near the entirety of his life to uncovering the secrets of the Dark Continent. On his way spreading the word of good faith and cheer with all those he was able, despite dubious health and overwhelming odds that frequently left the doctor in desperate straits. In Victorian Britain during the late 19th century, the mythical status of Dr. Livingstone, even posthumously, is nearly impossible to overstate. His inspiring success, growing from a young child spinning cotton threads in a mill to mapping the most dangerous recesses of Africa, gave hope to millions. Livingstone was furthermore of such moral character as to be beyond reproach, tirelessly advocating imperial reform as well as pioneering crusades of good will toward one's fellow man. And, as one will uncover in the learning of the life of this extraordinary man, he possessed the humbleness of a saint, and despite the humiliation sometimes encountered on his travels, he remained steadfast in his resolve and dedication.

Born on March 19th, 1813, Livingstone was encouraged at a young age to embrace education and be devoutly Christian and, even after working fourteen-hour days at the mill, studied tenaciously. These hardships taught him persistence, diligence and a deep and abiding respect for all working men, women and children. At the age of 26, Livingstone was hoping to travel to China but the First Opium War persuaded the London Missionary Society, of which Livingstone was a member, to travel to the West Indies instead to spread the faith. Dr. Livingstone travelled for years throughout Africa, and, in fact, was one of the first Westerners to make a transcontinental journey across Africa. This extraordinary feat was accomplished due to Livingstone's incredible capabilities of exploration and sheer charm and good will; he travelled lightly and was amazingly skilled at putting the numerous tribes, suspicious of outsiders to an alarming degree, at ease with his genuine nature and heartfelt goodwill.

Such was Livingstone's ability to put others at ease with jovial companionship and straightforward, kind speech that he was able to traverse dangerous lands without violent reprimands. Eschewing the traditional soldiers, rifles and armaments, Livingstone travelled with but a few porters and servants, and as such was able to assure the many formerly anti-Western populations that his intentions were of pure heart, as opposed to an imperialist incursion or slave-raiding party. Livingstone was a man of deep and abiding faith, and spoke most kindly to all who would listen concerning such matters, but never once forced his beliefs onto another; he respected the autonomy and opinion of others far too much to ever be anything but a gracious guest among their midst.

As Dr. Livingstone progressed, he believed God called him towards formalising routes of commercial trade deep within the heart of Africa, so as to aid in displacing the slave trade in favour of a more profitable and less barbaric economy, instead of merely preaching to the uninformed masses. As such, he resigned from the London Missionary Society in 1857. The Crown was impressed with Livingstone's dedication and accomplishments and appointed him to be Her Majesty's Counsel for the East Coast of Africa. At this point, he returned to South-Eastern Africa on his so-called "Zambezi Expedition" in order to formalise trade routes within the area. During this six-year period, despite the mounting of deserters and bodies, the latter including his own wife due to malaria, Livingstone pressed onwards, so intent was he on discovering the River Zambezi's secrets. His own physician called him *"... out of his mind and a most unsafe leader"* such was his perseverance and ceaseless drive to free the continent into a near era of understanding. Livingstone was indomitable: *"I am prepared to go anywhere, provided it be forward."*

By 1869, Livingstone's situation took a turn for the worse. He suffered terribly from pneumonia and the vast majority of his supplies were absconded away by duplicitous scoundrels. Even then, the jungles and marshlands saw fit to further deteriorate the doctor's condition, striking him down with cholera and horrendous tropic ulcers on his feet.

So desperate was his condition that he took to plying his works among the slavers themselves. Enthralled by the forthright nature of Livingstone they agreed to ferry him to Bambara. Still alive, Livingstone was able to take shelter before the beginning of the wet season, when overland travel, and indeed travel by waterway, is a dangerous venture.

With neither supplies nor funds, Livingstone needed to use his vast intellect and tenacious thirst for survival to resist the looming spectre of death. Allowing himself to be jeered, mocked and made into something of a local grotesque in exchange for sustenance, he willingly subjected himself to dining within a roped-off enclosure, stinking of faecal matter, sweat and grime. He endured terrible treatment in order to ensure his continued life. Livingstone was degraded into mere entertainment with a standard of living deplorable to anyone with a sense of decency. Men, women and children would travel from miles around to pelt the so-called pale-skin devil with bruised fruits and mouldy vegetables, which Livingstone was forced to partake in for his health, as he was too sick to work or travel.

All this Livingstone endured, and, in fact, encouraged, as a creative and admirable solution to his woes, and to avoid the uselessness of begging. Such suffering Livingstone endured merely strengthened his resolve, and he made a miraculous recovery in the squalid conditions of the backwater village. Alone and all but forgotten within the treacherous terrain of the jungles of Africa, his determination and indomitable countenance proved to be the victor in the face of overwhelming adversity, and Livingstone went on to be known as "Africa's greatest missionary," beloved by all who knew him and his works.

THE LEGENDARY
CROSS-COUNTRY TREK OF
HUGH GLASS

$\mathcal{O}$NE of the greatest frontier folk heroes of early America, Hugh Glass, was a fur trapper that did much to expand the knowledge of and trade within the American West. Born in Pennsylvania in 1780, Glass became a famed and highly skilled explorer; specifically within the watershed of the Upper Missouri River in what is present day the states of North Dakota, South Dakota and Montana. His tenacious attitude, canny wits fit for business and imposing demeanour, not to mention his great skills in hunting and survival, served him well throughout the course of his famed career. Indeed, one of the most startling journeys to have ever been recorded was a result of the indomitable spirit and astounding physical endurance of Glass, and this retelling only cements its well-earned status.

The journey began in 1822, with Glass responding to an advertisement, placed by one General William Ashley, which called for a corps of some one hundred men to travel the Missouri upriver in a fur trading venture. The men later came to be remembered as Ashley's Hundred. Several other noteworthy men included themselves amongst the corps, but their contributions were vastly overshadowed by that of Glass, who immediately proved himself to be a dedicated, ferocious trapper. Along the route, Glass and about a dozen men separated themselves from the main expeditionary force in order to relieve traders at Fort Henry, which was located at the mouth of the Yellowstone River. This detachment had plans to travel from the Missouri River up to the valley of the Grand River, which is located in present-day South Dakota. From there they would attempt to cross the valley to reach the Yellowstone, but Glass never made it to his destination.

In August of 1823, Glass was scouting ahead of his group in an effort to restock their provisions when he surprised a female grizzly bear and her two cubs hidden within the trees and uneven terrain of the forks of the Grand River. Glass immediately made to raise his loaded rifle, yet was unable to aim it in time to prevent the mother bear from charging him, her horrendous roar echoing through the landscape as she sought to defend her cubs from the intruder in her territory. She barrelled clumsily into Glass, her enormous weight lifting him from the ground and throwing him roughly aside. Glass, barely winded from the attack, sprang back up to his feet, knife in hand, and ran at the bear, the blade flashing in the broken sunlight of the clearing, as it sunk deep into the animal's thick flesh. The bear stood her ground, seemingly unaware of the assault, and raked her own claws as living steel across Glass' brawny, but unarmoured body.

Continually the two titans dove at one another, the firearm knocked out of reach in the initial confrontation. The repeated, expertly placed stabs and cuts from Glass' knife proved no mere stings, as exemplified by the free-flowing blood and copious wounds that now decorated the heaving monster, its cubs squalling from the sideline. Glass too was not left unscathed and remained upright and steady despite his back being degenerated into a mess of open wounds and exposed bone, sinew and muscle. Two of Glass' trapping partners, Fitzgerald and Bridger, heard the epic struggle emanating throughout the woodlands, and rushed to his aid. Before their coming upon the scene of the mighty contestants pitting their strength and will to survive against one another, Glass was able to land several blows at the bear's sensitive eyes. Blinded, enraged and rapidly dying, the enormous beast heaved itself in a last-ditch effort at Glass, its massive weight pinning him to the ground and knocking him senseless just as he drove his blade to the hilt into the creature's neck.

Fitzgerald and Bridger stumbled upon the battleground, aghast at the sight; the massive bear was unmoving, its chest no longer heaving with exertion, now but a prone mass of fur and meat in an indelicate repose on top of the body of Glass, whose shuddering gasps for air lent credence to his grasping for life. With great effort, the bear was shoved from atop Glass, who had been rendered unconscious and with but a tenuous thread to this world due to the terrible wounds he had sustained in his gladiatorial fight. The rest of the group caught up with the three as Glass' wounds were accounted for, and, truly, it was as if he had been mauled by a bear and won. Uncountable lacerations covered his form, with many deep, ragged cuts criss-crossing his torso and every limb. A leg had been shattered to pieces by the weight of the animal and, along his back; a number of ribs were broken and exposed to the elements. Still, Glass drew breath, but seemed to be on the verge of expiration. The leader of the group asked for volunteers to sit vigil for Glass and give him a proper burial, as his condition was deemed too sensitive to allow for his movement. Bridger and Fitzgerald volunteered for the solemn duty.

The pair began to dig what was planned to become the final resting place of Glass, amidst the stones and roots and scarred earth of his battleground. They tired quickly of the backbreaking labour with their meagre tools and decided to shamefully remove themselves from their self-imposed duty. Taking Glass' rifle, knife and all of his other sundries and equipment, they left Glass to supposedly die alone in the woods as the two ventured to re-join the group further ahead. Glass was left with little more than ripped clothing splattered with the blood of man and beast alike. Bridger and Fitzgerald, after reaching their team, erroneously, irresponsibly, and downright maliciously reported that they had been interrupted by an attack by savage natives and furthermore claimed that Glass had died shortly before their flight. Their lies were not questioned, and they proceeded onwards on their previous undertaking.

Miraculously, in spite of sustaining injuries that would have killed most men on the spot, Glass was able to regain consciousness. He found himself completely and utterly alone, a decomposing, skinless bear several feet away at his side, and in enough pain to leave any normal human in a gibbering, worthless state. He could smell his wounds festering and knew his leg was nigh useless, shattered as it was. With rough calculation, he found himself about 200 miles from Fort Kiowa, the nearest American settlement. Grossly disfigured, alone and without arms or equipment, Glass resolved himself to undertake one of the most extraordinary journeys to have ever been completed.

Using his vast knowledge of survival, navigation and rudimentary medicine, Glass bound and set his own leg with nothing but sticks and strips of cloth. He used the raw, poorly conditioned bear skin that had been placed over him as a shroud as some meagre protection from the elements, and began to crawl. He soon came across a decaying tree stump, which proved to be a great boon to a man of such iron will as Glass. He heaved himself against it, resting his mutilated back against its soft, exposed innards. The sickly sweet smell of infection signalled the maggots that a rare treat was to be served. They swarmed his open wounds, infesting him thoroughly, eating away at the diseased flesh and in the process treating gangrene. Death, which he had so narrowly avoided at the jaws and claws of the mother bear, was once again fooled. Recovering, Glass headed south to the Cheyenne River to avoid hostile natives, a six-week endurance crawl at his slow, deliberate pace.

Surviving on a diet of berries and roots primarily, Glass gained strength along his route. Once he even came upon a downed bison calf being worried on by two wolves. Despite his weakness he was able to drive them away from their kill and feasted on the meat. Thus gaining much needed strength for his travel. After reaching the Cheyenne River, Glass fastened together a makeshift raft and utilised it to float downriver, using the easily seen Thunder Butte as a landmark to navigate by. Along the river, he encountered several Native Americans that, to his relief, proved to be friendly. They procured a fresh bear skin that they sewed onto Glass' back to protect his still exposed wounds and provided him much needed equipment and food. Newly stocked and armed, Glass made it to Fort Kiowa in a much better condition, infuriated at his abandonment.

After recuperating fully at Fort Kiowa, Glass set out to take revenge on Fitzgerald and Bridger, the two men that left him to die. For a seasoned tracker such as Glass, this was an easy feat. He discovered Bridger at the Yellowstone River, near the mouth of the Bighorn River. Bridger fell to his knees at the sight of wrath incarnate that was Glass, pleading for his life to be spared. Glass was moved by the young man's cries and took pity. Bridger being only 19 and easily swayed to near any course of action was spared a brutal death. Thankful to the point of tears, Bridger swore to never forget the gracious action and kindness that Glass had displayed.

Fitzgerald, being older and more devious, proved more difficult to locate. Glass tracked him doggedly and eventually found him to have joined the United States Army. Fitzgerald was white as a sheet at the sight of what was most assuredly a ghost. Glass was doomed to have died, he had assumed, but there he was. All rage and fury! Glass forcefully took the rifle that Fitzgerald had stolen from him and threatened to kill him on the spot with the very weapon, but after consideration stayed his hand. The murder of a soldier, even in the name of vengeance, was worthy of execution, and Glass had not persevered only to die at the end of an axe. He allowed Fitzgerald to live, but his point had been made - do not cross such a man that has killed a grizzly bear in hand to hand combat.

THE NEPALESE GOD OF WAR AND HIS ASSAULT ON DEOTHAL

$\mathcal{A}$n outstanding combative ability, rigorous loyalty to his comrades and an unsurpassed fearlessness of death - it is these traits that exemplify the Gurkhas, an exalted collection of military units that draw men from the indigenous people of Nepal. Their outstanding military prowess is legendary the world wide, and they have served with brutal efficiency across the globe, for, although they meet many of the standards for mercenaries as set forth by the Geneva Convention, they retain an exemption that bears similarity to that of the French Foreign Legion. For centuries, these truly fearless men have clashed with privateers, mercenaries, militia and professional soldiers, consistently showing an unparallelled capacity for both brutality and unquestionable loyalty on the battlefield.

One such man was Bhakti Thapa. Born to inauspicious beginnings in an impoverished shepherding family high in the Himalaya Mountains in 1741, Bhakti was made of an iron that only tempered as he aged. He was extremely athletic as a child, able to scale the mountainous terrain effortlessly as he herded his sheep, despite the altitude leaving the air so thin that most people would be left sputtering and breathless. As Bhakti grew older, he aspired to leave his craggy home behind and join the army, which he did upon turning eighteen.

Bhakti served with surpassing distinction for nearly sixty years. He quickly rose to a position of command during the bloody circumvention of the British East India Company in 1767. The Kingdom of Gorkha, located close to present-day Nepal, began a period of great expansion wherein they invaded the Kathmandu Valley, renamed the entire combined region the Great Empire of Nepal, and then easily destroyed some 2,500 British troops that had been sent to quell what they called a mere "native uprising." From there, war reigned throughout the subcontinent, and Bhakti and his compatriots battled the Sikhs in Punjab, the Chinese in Tibet and the British in India for decades. Only through being severely outnumbered on a front were the battle-hardened Gurkhas beaten back.

Although Nepal eventually settled its differences with Punjab and Tibet, entering into an uneasy peace with the neighbouring countries, animosity continued between Nepal and the British East India Company, mainly due to Nepal's refusal of British trade routes through Nepal. This refusal kindled an explosion of defiance when, in 1814, The British East India Company declared open war on Nepal and punctuated their declaration with the mustering of over 20,000 men to subdue Nepal and carve a gore-slicked swathe through the country. These were no peasants and ill-equipped dregs. No, this was a professional military force, contending with great aplomb for the most fearsome in the world, and near the height of its power and influence. For the vast majority of targets the British East India Company set their sights on, a rapid surrender would be expected at best, or at worst a massacre at the end of gun and cannon, bayonet and sabre. The Gurkhas, despite being terribly under-equipped and outnumbered, refused to succumb to the will of the British East India Company. Bhakti Thapa and his Gurkhas sharpened their kukri daggers, the iconic curved knives for which they are known, packed hastily melted ball bearings and nails into their shotguns, and prepared for the onslaught.

As Nepal attempted to defend itself, Bhakti Thapa initially ordered the securing of his mountain strongholds. Using elephants to drag cannons up the rocky slopes, he hoped that a combination of horrid disease, breath-taking altitude and copious gunshot wounds would turn the British advance. These strategies did stem the tide, at first, but the British displayed only an iron will, for any inkling of fear would threaten their stranglehold on the Indian subcontinent. The British, led by the outstanding General Sir David Ochterloney, used their superior numbers to deftly divide the smaller Nepalese forces, extinguishing them piece by piece despite horrendous losses. Bit by bit, the Gurkhas, with all of their martial might, lost ground to the large, disciplined and quickly recovering British forces.

Eventually, the British outmanoeuvred the Gurkhas and seized an easily defended, high-altitude fortress called Deothal, placed deep within the mountains. A full frontal assault was the only feasible move to retake the fortress. Although surely a suicide mission, Bhakti knew it was imperative to reclaim the stronghold if the war was to be won. And so, he chose 2,000 troops nearly as imposing as himself, even now at seventy-four years of age, and made way to retake Deothal by sheer force.

At 4:00 AM on April 16th, 1815, Bhakti Thapa and 2,000 of the most menacing warriors on the planet rushed forth from their camp situated below Deothal and, bellowing war cries, attempted to storm the fortress. Deothal would not be easily assailed. It was chock full with over 3,500 British and Indian soldiers, and they had thought to arm themselves with a battery of, at the time, ultra-modern six-pounder cannons. The cannons proved to be incredibly effective, as the Gurkhas were mowed down *"like wheat"* by one account.

Despite hails of musket balls and grapeshot, the Gurkhas rushed ahead fearlessly through the treacherous terrain, climbing adroitly like the Sherpas that many had been raised as. Their battle lines began to rip apart, but Bhakti, leading the charge from the front, called out to encourage his fellows, and they raced ahead unimpeded into the leaden maw of Deothal. Against impossible odds, Bhakti and his men reached the artillery battery through an astounding climb, and Bhakti, levelling his double-barrelled shotgun, discharged it at the nearest artillery officer, a look of surprise frozen onto his face before clambering unceremoniously to the floor.

All but six of the gunners were wounded or killed in the initial formation of a toehold at Deothal, but the British rallied a second line of defence against the Gurkhas, who appeared more like demons than men with their bloodied knives and bone-chilling war cries. Once the British infantry had formed up, a volley of gunfire resounded as the musket balls impacted the mostly unarmoured Gurkhas, then the British rushed forward with their bayonets. The Gurkhas, already having discharged their shotguns, and with no time to reload their improvised ammunition, fought back with kukri and sword, screaming their oaths and curses amidst the stabbing and slashing. This began the most horrendous session of hand-to-hand combat the British East India Company would ever need to endure.

The battle raged for nearly an hour more. For every Gurkha that fell in the fight, another two British or Indian troops fell with him, but the Gurkhas had suffered enormous casualties on the initial climb, and, though their resolve was as steel, their numbers were low, and slowly their initial advantage from surprise gave way to the protracted fighting of superior numerical advantage. The Gurkha leader, Bhakti Thapa, by now he had slain near a dozen men, had suffered greatly. Blood blossomed through his once clean linens, and a weariness crept into his aged limbs that softened his blows, slowed his parries, and dulled his reactions. Opportunity found itself embodied in a Brown Bess, a popular muzzle-loading smoothbore, for its wielder was able to step forward from the chaos, aim at point-blank range at Bhakti's heaving chest, and pierce his heart with a musket ball, killing him before his body slumped on top of the mixture of dead and dying men circling him. Their commander, once so strong and hale, now seen dead, broke the will of the Gurkhas remaining, and they began to fall back. Deothal held strong.

General Ochterloney, impressed by the fighting prowess of Bhakti, treated the body with great respect. He had the body wrapped in a shawl and returned to the Nepalese lines, and both armies gathered in solemnity as his body was placed on a funeral pyre and burned amidst the carnage of the battlefield. With Bhakti Thapa's death, the war ended a mere month later, and the British East India Company seized control of one-third of Nepal in the process. However, so impressed were they with the Gurkhas' fighting spirit and tenacious blood thirst, that the Gurkhas were recruited to fight alongside the British. This would prove to be an enviable position, for the Gurkhas offered a great advantage to conflicts the world over, including wars in India, Germany and even the Falkland Islands.

In Nepal today, Deothal Battle Day is celebrated as a national holiday. On this day, the Nepalese people celebrate their unified, undaunted spirit. Twice a year, a Hindu priest sacrifices a pig at a shrine near Bhakti's former home in honour of his memory; there, seven broadswords and seven kukris that belonged to him hang, symbolising his unmatched skill in the dealing of death. Bhakti Thapa is officially recognised as a National Hero of Nepal, an honour which includes only a dozen people. This prestigious place in the collective memory of the Nepalese people, and the continued prowess of the Gurkhas, ensures that his actions continue to be remembered.

THE BLIND FIGHT OF
KING JOHN OF BOHEMIA

"ISCRETION is the better part of valour" some claim, but such idioms fell upon the ears of King John nearing the Battle of Crécy as though he were as deaf as he was blind. The progression of his life - from his royal birth in Luxembourg in 1296, his marriage and ascent to power in 1310, ordainment as a prince-elector of the Holy Roman Empire and subsequent abandonment of the administration of Bohemia in favour of travel and worldly knowledge by 1325, loss of eyesight from ophthalmia in 1336 whilst crusading in Lithuania, and allegiance to King Philip VI of France in the Hundred Years' War - had brought him to this, the outskirts of Crécy-en-Ponthieu in Northern France in August of 1346.

King John's loyal and trusted eyes advised him of the opposing English encampment - infantry, men-at-arms, crossbowmen, archers, and light cavalry in great numbers, well-armed, well-armoured and well-supplied, not to forget several ribaldis, an early artillery piece, stationed atop the hill. The English, well entrenched to the north of Crécy-en-Ponthieu on a small hill, enclosed by the River Maye and the forest of Crécy, presented a formidable presence for the odd 12,000 men-at-arms, several thousand Genoese crossbow-toting mercenaries and multitudes of common infantrymen the French commanders had at their disposal. The English forces, by virtue of the defender, were well rested and prepared for the oncoming battle, with well-divided battle lines and a system of ditches, pits and caltrops to disrupt enemy cavalry action. The French army, commanded by King Philip VI himself, was given no time for rest. Upon the arrival of the lumbering mass of men to the field, they were immediately arrayed for battle, lacking their pavises, large wooden shields which were the only protection against the English bolts.

The battle progressed poorly due to the haste of King Philip VI, and when the lines were drawn in what later proved to be one of the most decisive battles of the Hundred Years' War, it was clear that the French were in a precarious situation. The mercenary crossbowmen proved ineffective due to a thunderstorm during their six league march earlier that day and were disrupted and slaughtered without mercy. First by the longbow men of the English, and then, once routed, their nobles mounted on horseback. Giovanni Villani, famed Florentine and chronicler, wrote an account of the death witnessed:

52

"The English guns cast iron balls by means of fire... They made a noise like thunder and caused much loss in men and horses... The Genoese were continually hit by the archers and the gunners... [by the end of the battle], the whole plain was covered by men struck down by arrows and cannon balls."

The French cavalry charged following this terrible massacre. Hampered by the terrain and mounting heaps of bodies, they were beaten back repeatedly until finally, the English lines unbroken, they were forced to retreat from their strong formations and quit the field.

This is not the tale of the failings of French wartime doctrine, nor is it concerned overly with the inadequate commandership of King Philip VI, but instead with the bravery and honour that King John demanded upon himself. At the age of fifty, and blind for a decade at this point, King John had nothing to offer in the realm of martial prowess. Yet, when he heard of Lord Charles, his own flesh and blood, his treasured son, pressing forth into the fray, King John ordered his subordinates to facilitate his own contribution beyond mere sightless generalship. Enfeebled as he was, King John yearned to spur his men to victory by his presence on the battlefield, and, more importantly in his view, to make certain that his son, and later successor as Charles VI, Holy Roman Emperor, was unharmed.

Gathering his most trusted and beloved compatriots, King John spoke gravely but with great care, asking their aid to bring him to the front lines so that he may strike but one stroke with his sword at minimum, thus solidifying the cause of the perception of others as to his fearlessness and self-sacrifice. Tearfully, and with heavy hearts, his companions swore to aid in this endeavour. In preparation, King John sat on his war steed, armed and armoured as befitting his high station. The reins of the horse's bridle were tied to the next nearest, and so on, to make certain that none were left behind in the perilous press forward. Trusting his mount to make the best path, King John spurred him onwards and ahead of his retinue. First a slow walk through the encampment, then a brisk trot past the French lines, and then, with the hot-blooded shudder of his steed beneath him and the war cries of the French and English alike, blindly charged into a heedless gallop to meet certain death.

John, so enamoured was he with the pounding of hooves and the whizzing of missiles through the darkness of his blank eyes, raised sword and shield, the latter bearing his crest, a pair of black wings, and it seemed as though Death himself took pause in his reaping to allow his own champion a turn at the scythe. The king, and in turn his men, pushed perilously forward, arrows and bolts missing by inches as they crashed into the lines of the English, bodies falling all around, punctured, cut and pummelled beyond recognition. King John roared with unabated fury and glee, slashing back and forth, and by virtue of his chaotic stance and fearsome beast found himself deflecting the meagre resistance presented to the blind man, as indeed the opposition had the rallied Frenchmen to contend with as well.

Valiantly he sallied forth, and the touch of Death was on his blade as miraculously he struck the scurrying English, for his allies, with great wisdom, gave him wide berth. Again and again his blows rained down, more often striking only empty air as his mount crushed with hooves and teeth alike, but also still connecting a multitude of times, whether that be against armour or flesh it was difficult to ascertain. The flagging English regained their wits and their superior positioning and began to push back, legions of spearmen like enormous, malleable porcupines skewering anything in their wake. Unaware of the increased danger, King John continued to slash madly atop his horse, deafened further by the blood lust that seized his mind, and his dearest friends, unwilling to leave John behind, closed ranks near him and sought to cut down five for every one of their company that fell.

Inevitably disaster struck, as the king's steed was impaled thrice in short order. With a crazed neigh dying in its blood-filled throat, the horse and King John, intricately bound and strapped to his creature, fell thunderously. The king cried out in agony, his call a worthy substitute for his mount's missing breath, for his leg was pinned and crushed beneath the massive weight of that once noble stallion. Yet still, with mud and blood intermingling in his mouth, he refused to lay silent and await death, and continued to stab all around, despite the weariness of his sword arm. This could not continue, for Death stalked this hill, and King John was slain with neither fanfare nor ceremony on that hilltop by unknown footmen, and, in their own turn, the remainder of his men followed suit, for they refused to leave their liege whilst air still filled their lungs.

That next day, as the English troops made an account of the dead, King John was found, sword clenched in hand in death as it was in life, with wide eyes seeing as much now as the decade before. Arrayed all around were the bodies of his closest men, unwilling to abandon their king at any point before or after his ceasing of life. And, indeed, all were connected, for their bridles still were tied as before, and all still solidly on the backs of their expired horses. Despite the overwhelming odds presented to this fine assortment, all fought with valour, and, following in their king's example, all fought like King John of Bohemia.

THE TALE OF UNSINKABLE
SAM AND HIS LUCKINESS
THROUGHOUT THE
SECOND WORLD WAR

*H*ISTORY books are filled with stories of heroic men, daring women and all around inspiring figures living and excelling throughout the ages. Far fewer in number are the creatures of fur and fang, feather and talon, or scale and claw. Our animal companions too are capable of greatness, and of exemplifying the qualities we hold dear in our fellows. Courage, tenacity, perseverance, and, above all, the capability to overcome the impossible and to be immortalised in our collective memory - these can be displayed both in man and beast. One of these creatures was an unlikely feline, whose survival time and again defied all attempts of explanation.

When the German battleship *Bismarck* set sail on May 18th, 1941, it embarked on its first and only mission, Operation Rheinübung. On its departure, a black and white patched cat was also on board, belonging at the time to some unknown crewman. Either for companionship or to aid in keeping the rodent infestations to a minimum, perhaps a combination of both, this possibly nameless cat set forth for war with his more aware compatriots. The life of the *Bismark* was doomed to be short-lived, for on May 27th, the ship engaged in a ferocious battle at sea, where it sustained heavy damage at the end of the opposition's guns, and began to sink with surprising haste. The skeleton crew of its original 2,200 sailors tried mightily to stem the rising waters, but to no avail, despite their herculean efforts.

The *Bismark* dipped beneath the surface, taking with it corpses and men struggling for their life. Hours later, as rescue efforts went underway, 115 members of the original crew were found and fished from the icy grasp of the sea. Our furry friend, alas, was not amongst them. By sheer chance, the *HMS Cossack*, on its way back home to Britain, happened to come across a most peculiar sight as it passed through the wreckage of the *Bismark*: a patchwork cat, floating serenely on a board, calm, dry and seeming to be wholly content with the world. After bringing the cat on board, the cat was quite agreeable, the crew of the *Cossack*, being unaware of whatever name he had before now, decided to name their new mascot "Oscar".

Oscar served dutifully on the *Cossack* for the next several months, proving himself rather valuable in catching rats and the attention of its sailors. During this time, the *Cossack* carried out its convoy escort duties within the North Atlantic Ocean and Mediterranean Sea. On October 24th, 1941, the *Cossack* was travelling with a convoy from the Strait of Gibraltar to the United Kingdom, a rather uneventful journey at this point, when disaster struck. German U-boats policed the waters like sharks, and the convoy seemed to be defenceless. One submarine, *U-563*, torpedoed the *Cossack* in a surprise assault, crippling the vessel immediately to the point of nearly sinking. The crew rushed to save the ship, and barely managed to pump out enough water to make rudimentary repairs while the attack was fended off. To prevent further unnecessary casualties, the crew of the *Cossack* was transferred to the *HMS Legion* and an attempt was made to tow the badly listing *Cossack* back to Gibraltar for much-needed repairs at a dry dock located there. En route, the seas began to rise, with frozen rain pelting the ships. The situation became so dire that all hope of recovering the *Cossack* to full strength was abandoned, and the tow was slipped, causing the ship to sink the very next day. The initial explosion caused by the torpedo resulted in 159 deaths of which none feline. Oscar was brought aboard the *Legion* with the remainder of the crew and ferried to a shore establishment at Gibraltar.

After his arrival at Gibraltar, Oscar, now nicknamed "Unsinkable Sam" by the amazed crew, was soon transferred to the *HMS Ark Royal*, a massive aircraft carrier that, with great irony, had been instrumental in the destruction of the *Bismark*. Here too, Sam would encounter a most unfortunate occurrence. The *Ark Royal*, returning from Malta on November 14th, 1941, came into the sights of another German submarine. This one designated *U-81*. The *Ark Royal* was helpless to avoid the racing torpedo, which impacted violently, causing a breach of the hull that gushed seawater into its shorn compartments. Attempts were made to tow the *Ark Royal* back to Gibraltar for repairs, but the inflow of water was impossible to hold back and the carrier rolled over and sank beneath the waves some thirty miles from the shoreline. Due to the slow rate at which the *Ark Royal* sunk, all but one of the crew surviving the initial strike could be saved. Those survivors, including Sam himself, who was found to be unharmed yet quite irate while clinging to a bit of plank by a small vessel, were transferred to the *HMS Lightning*, and then once more the *HMS Legion*, which happened to be that same *Legion* that had earlier quartered Sam after his initial confrontation with death on the *Cossack*.

After the *Ark Royal's* inevitable sinking, a life at sea no longer seemed to be in Sam's future. He was transferred officially to the office of the Governor of Gibraltar, and then much later sent to the United Kingdom, to live out the remainder of the war peacefully at a seaman's home in Belfast. In 1955, Sam's eventful life came to an end as he died of natural causes. During the war, both the *HMS Legion* and the *HMS Lightning* would sink due to enemy action, the former in 1942, and the latter in 1943. It seems as though Death himself attempted to claim Sam's life on those vessels of war over and over without success. Sam, however, would only relent to his cold embrace on the solid ground that was his birthright. Today, "Unsinkable Sam" is forever enshrined in a portrait at the National Maritime Museum in Greenwich, so that anyone may gaze upon this paragon of indomitable will in the face of drowning on the open sea.

THE HEROISM OF ARLAND D. WILLIAMS, JR. UPON THE POTOMAC RIVER

$\mathcal{G}$REATNESS need not be earned over the course of a lifetime. While there are many men and women of legendary status that have attained such acclaim due the actions of an entire life bereft of the mundane, there are numerous others that, in one brief, defining moment, throw off their airs of obscurity and exemplify the true heroic virtues in a time of great crisis: selflessness, charity, and self-sacrifice. We speak highly of those that perform great feats of valour, honour or glory. Even greater is the man that seeks not fame, nor recognition, but only to serve others at the cost of himself. One such, formerly unassuming man, that we remember with heartfelt words for acts of altruism , is Arland D. Williams, Jr.

Williams never seemed destined to be a hero. Born into a typical family in Illinois in 1935, he went on to attend The Citadel, a military college in South Carolina. This is notable due to the Citadel's rigorous swimming requirements, which filled Williams with trepidation. Never a strong swimmer, Williams had a grave fear of the water and believed this to be a failing worthy of his dismissal. Nonetheless, Williams succeeded due to his persevering attitude, and after graduating, served his two years at a stateside post with, perhaps not distinction, but a quiet dignity. Afterwards he went into banking, and in time became a mildly successful bank examiner. It seemed as though Williams was on track to finish out a normal life, with never an opportunity, nor perhaps even a desire, to showcase the best of what one man has to offer to his fellow man. Circumstances, however, contrived to deny Williams this attempt at a mundane existence.

The date of January 13th, 1982, brought with it a terrible bout of freezing temperatures and icy winds to the Washington National Airport. Despite these horrendous hazards, Air Florida decided to press through with their flights, one happening to be carrying seventy-four passengers and five crew members from this origin to Fort Lauderdale, Florida. Amongst the passengers was Williams, who, despite his fear upon spying the icy runways and frozen wings of the plane felt assured with the guarantees of the flight attendants that everything would be safe for a secure take-off. With a sigh of relief, Williams stowed his carry-on baggage in the overhead compartment and seated himself in his cramped rear seat on the none-too-large plane, clearly meant only for minor domestic flights. During a delay of nearly half an hour, Williams thought intently on demanding to be let off the plane, as it idly sat on the slick tarmac awaiting its clearance. His apprehension of the impending flight was apparent on his face as he reconsidered, and then began to think of it again.

The plane began to slowly roll down the runway at 3:59 PM, after being towed by chains from the departure zone. Williams' knuckles turned white as he gripped the hard plastic of his armrests, crowding out his disgruntled neighbour. Faster and faster, the soon-to-be airborne plane trundled downwards, its proportionally small wheels gaining little traction on the frozen asphalt. Sliding forth on its predestined path, the pilots of Flight 90 began to worry, their various gauges and meters reporting a troubling conclusion: the plane was not gaining lift as fast as it needed to reach the minimum for an appropriate take-off. In hushed, measured voices they quickly discussed their options in the span of a few seconds: continue onwards and hope to gain enough momentum to achieve flight, or abort the take-off, which at minimum would cause the passengers and the airline major headaches, or at worst would leave the plane sliding off the edge of the runway and potentially damaging it. Despite their hesitation, they were pressed onwards by the command tower. A fatal miscalculation on the hands of, it would later be defined, not one man, but the hubris, ineptitude, and ill luck of many.

The plane's velocity remained too low for the ease of anyone aware as the end of the runway was approaching. The pilots did everything in their power to squeeze out as much lift as they could from the icy wings, but to little effect, and their aircraft was only barely skimming the surface as the runway ended. Rising up twenty, forty, sixty feet in the air, warnings blazed in the cockpit as the pilots struggled valiantly against the rebellious controls, the plane wobbling in the frigid air as it streaked through the capital. Its passengers, well aware of the emergency, began to panic wildly as trees and buildings rushed past the windows, just out of reach of the wings. With a shocking lurch the nose began to tilt downward sharply as passers-by either fled in fear or stood stock still in surprise.

This auspicious day the steady traffic passing across the collection of five bridges over the Potomac River, known as the 14th Street Bridges, was typical. Unfortunately, the bridge for northbound traffic lay directly in the path of Flight 90. The stalled plane thundered downwards as its screaming passengers clung to their seat belts and loved ones, unsure whether this would be their final moment. With the last dregs of control, the pilots did all they could to steer the floundering craft towards the Potomac River, away from the more populated areas, in a last-ditch effort to minimise the damage of their impending crash.

Within merely a few seconds, at 4:01 PM, the nose of the plane collided with a stupendous cacophony with the bridge, shearing it in half and perforating the landscape within a hundred meters with crunched, shredded metal. The plane smashed through the four-lane bridge with explosive force, taking with it a truck and six cars as they made their commute - painlessly, we can hope, killing four motorists in total, while injuring a score of others. The plane's momentum was slowed precipitously, but even the bridge could not halt the path of this flying behemoth as its twisted, shattered fuselage broke through and smashed with a roar into the freezing body of the Potomac River, sending forth terrifying waves of ice and water as the demolished body of Flight 90 plunged into its murky depths.

Inside the cabin, chaos reigned as everything but the back quarter crumpled into an almost unrecognisable heap immediately as the plane began to submerge. Williams, amazingly, remained conscious despite the massive impact and was able to just barely free himself from the tangled seatbelt as the freezing water poured over him. Blinded, deafened, drowning, Williams struggled to right himself as the groaning mass shuddered due to the pressure of the water. He groped along the remainder of the sides and seats hurriedly, desperate for any clue to his salvation, when he felt a rift in the plane, brought about by the fierce collision. His lungs burning, yearning for air, he pulled his weight through and shot to the surface, taking in sporadic, yet deeply satisfying breaths of frigid air.

Williams was finally able to take stock of himself, and after brief contemplation found that he was almost completely unharmed, as far as he could tell, while bobbing next to the tail section of the plane, which jutted abruptly from the water. Looking around, he saw only five fellow passengers clinging to life in the wide river with him; none others surfaced to join their numbers. The wide, ice-choked river quickly had its edges swarmed by onlookers, as emergency services arrived on scene to survey the damage. News cameras looked on helplessly from the bridge as the tail section, which had broken off from the main body, slowly made its way to the depths. Passers-by, the first arrivals to the scene, attempted a makeshift rope to haul in the survivors, but this proved ineffective, as none were able to brave the freezing temperatures of the Potomac

Finally, hope arrived at 4:20 PM when Eagle 1, a United States Park Police helicopter, arrived to assist in the rescue efforts. The helicopter was not outfitted to properly engage in rescue operations, and, in fact, was scarcely big enough for the pilot and paramedic riding aboard. The pilot flew in close overhead, its rotors stirring up a harsh wind and introducing a chop to the once calm waters, and tossed a towline below, intent on dragging it from the wreckage to the shore. Williams, knowing that others needed attention more than himself, assisted in passing the line to two of the most critically injured survivors, and they were towed, one at a time, to safety.

Eagle 1 returned several times to tow people ashore, even going so low as to dip its skids into the waters, and while many lives were saved, two unfortunately slipped their lines and sank beneath the waters, not to be seen again. Over and over, Williams helped provide the safety of everyone else before himself, passing off the line that dropped down to him for the betterment of strangers. He knew time was limited: with each passing moment, the remaining section of the Boeing 737 shifted further and further beneath the waterline, and the bitter cold numbed his mind and body. He denied the lifeline again and again to make sure that everyone else was safe. As the last remaining passenger, short of Williams himself, was brought to the shore the tail finally slipped underwater. Williams, seeing that he had saved all that he could, went with it.

To this day, Williams is remembered as a giver of life, but even greater than that, one that sacrificed his own life so that others might live. Without staying his innate desire for survival, all those other people in the water might have perished, sinking beneath the waves as he doomed himself to do. Now he is celebrated, a paragon of the best man can be in the direst of circumstances. Arland D. Williams, Jr. exemplified what it means to have true empathy. Not merely for those you love and care for, but for complete strangers that you have never met before, and may never see again.

The Retribution of Xerxes' upon the Dardanelles

*I*N 482 BC, the massive armies of Xerxes I were poised to sweep into Persia, after the outright subjugation of Greece at his command during the Greco-Persian Wars. Archers, spearmen, cavalry and horrifying monstrosities of war were prepped and ready to be unleashed with just a wave of his regal hand. There was but one obstacle, even for the God-like entity that was Xerxes, which gave pause. Hellespont, the Sea of Helle, more commonly named the Dardanelles in recent times, prevented progress. This narrow strait, commonly named one of the most dangerous the world over, many a time smashed ships, bridges and men alike on its rocky outcroppings, if it didn't drag them down to its roiling depths first.

As Xerxes could not part the waters or raise dry land from the seabed, he settled for the mundane solution: construct two pontoon bridges across its width at the, even then, ancient city of Abydos, across from which lies the city of Sestus at slightly more than a nautical mile in distance. Xerxes set his vast ranks of engineers and builders on the task. They in turn ordered men to behave as locusts and devour what had not already been consumed by the rest of Xerxes' sea of men. Countless spools of rope joined with the lumber of a dozen forests, not to forget the vast quantity of incidentals required in the construction of a project of this magnitude. Weeks of endless labour caused the bridges to take form rapidly. Despite the losses of hundreds of lives into the raging currents below, the progress of Xerxes' bridges could not be impeded, as there were five men to replace any one lost. As the completion neared, the armies became restless with the lack of conquest, but prepared themselves nonetheless for the death incarnate they would unleash upon the feeble Persian defences.

At last, it was done, and the pontoon bridges stretched the entire width of the strait unimpeded, its rough construction nonetheless strong enough to bear the weight of man and animal alike, and Xerxes intended to snake them across in an unending train stretching for miles. However, even Xerxes' self-imposed divine nature could not hinder Nature itself, and at the completion, as plans moved into action to begin the crossing, the skies darkened, and the waters below frothed and boiled with the hellish rage that only the uncaring, primal forces can draw upon themselves. The winds blew harshly, and sheets of rain fell upon the strait with an intensity few had experienced before. The bridges bucked dozens of feet in the air as the waves crashed through the length of the strait, and then crashed back down again with enough force to drown out the thunder. They strained and warped, battered and beaten into submission, and were smashed to pieces by the waves and rocks. In just a few hours, weeks of blood, sweat and tears were washed away by the implacable storm, and even Xerxes' rage paled in comparison to the fury it unleashed on the hapless crews.

The morning dawned on the horrendous sight: choppy waves as empty as the day Xerxes had approached them, with bits of his construction dotting the shores, a testament to the destruction of the previous day. The many encampments quickly received word of the storm's ravaging and grew uneasy at the thought of Xerxes' eminent wrath. And wrath there was, for Xerxes was thrown into a fit of madness confirming his mythical status of being a demented God. His first act, once he regained a measure of composure, was to behead all those responsible for building the now shattered bridges, resulting in hundreds of pikes with fresh, bloody banners. This act of poorly directed vengeance was not enough to sate Xerxes, as he believed that the sea itself had also attempted to defy his rightful claim to Persia. He decided that the sea should share in the punishment.

That same day, Xerxes meted out his own absurd version of justice. For the atrocity that had been committed against his forces, he demanded harsh retribution, such that any mortal would perish surely from his wounds. As with any prisoner, the seas would need to be physically subjugated, and Xerxes ordered his men to throw dozens of fetters into the water, the crude metal sinking rapidly to the bottom, unhindered. If any men had doubt about the efficacy of Xerxes' plan, none dared to voice it, for fear of their own head being added to the collection he had already accrued thanks to the contributions of the builders.

The strait properly subdued, Xerxes ordered his most fearsome guard, armed with jewel-encrusted whips, to its shores, their conduct as fierce and determined as their master's. At the wave of Xerxes' hand, as he sat in his shaded palanquin, the guardsmen began to shout curses, demeaning the strait for its petty defiance of Xerxes' divine will, and whipped at the waves as they came crashing in. Three hundred swings were given in total and each one as ineffective as the last. The spray of the waves was barely parted by the harsh blows, but this act was duly fulfilled, and Xerxes was pleased to watch his highly skilled warriors slice at the shoreline.

As the men retreated from the waters, spent from their exertions, Xerxes enacted his last act of retribution. An enormous fire, built of the smashed bridges that were once to be the death of Greece, was built, and irons placed deep in its heart and heated to red-hot temperatures. That accomplished, the irons were grabbed, and Xerxes' men waded deep into the strait and plunged the irons into the seawater, the steam from the thrust mingling with the mist of the oncoming waves to form a distinct haze near the shoreline. Xerxes intended to mark the Dardanelles as cowed by the righteous anger that he unleashed, and succeeded in little more than soaking a number of his guard through, and leaving many of them confused as to what exactly had been accomplished. Nonetheless, Xerxes had demonstrated his mastery over Nature, and many of his more devout soldiers were heartened by the overt, yet bizarre, display of sovereign power.

The Inspiring Self-Sacrifice of Captain Lawrence "Titus" Oates

$\mathcal{T}$HOSE of English descent are renowned around the world for their enduring stoicism in the face of overwhelming adversity. A "stiff upper lip" as it is colloquially called at times, Captain Lawrence Oates came to embody this attribute over his many years of service, culminating in the greatest act one man can perform for another.

Born in Putney, London, England, in the year of 1880, he attended South Lynn School, an army preparatory school, as he came of age. In 1898, Oates was commissioned into the 3rd Militia Battalion of the West Yorkshire Regiment. Serving with distinction, coupled with a great love of horses, later led Oates to participating honourably in the Second Boer War as a junior officer in the 6th Inniskilling Dragoons, an ancient and well-regarded cavalry order. In March of 1901, Oates suffered grievously from a gunshot wound to his thigh, with its eventual healing leaving his left leg a full inch shorter than his right. In the skirmish in which the injury was incurred, Oates was twice called upon to surrender, to which he replied both times with *"We came to fight, not to surrender."* For his actions, he was recommended the Victoria Cross and Oates was brought to public attention for his deeds. From there he ascended rapidly to Lieutenant, and then later Captain, and served in Ireland, Egypt and India, with his prowess only expanding further with each conquest.

In 1910, Oates volunteered to join Robert Falcon Scott's expedition, entitled the Terra Nova Expedition, to the South Pole. Scott, a Royal Navy officer and leader of the now complete Discovery Expedition, which was the first official British exploration of the Antarctic Region in over 60 years, was impressed with Oates military record and renowned horsemanship. Not to mention Oates' offering of £1,000 (which by current reckonings would muster a contribution equivalent to greater than £50,000) to aid in financing the expedition, which would go far in realising this outlandish dream. As such, Oates was hired on to tend to the ponies that were to haul sledges during the initial creation of larders at strategic points for later use, as well as the first leg of the actual journey. In time, Oates was furthermore selected as one of the five-man crew that would make the trek all the way to the South Pole.

Unfortunately, Oates and Scott came to words, and at times nearly blows, over stark differences in managerial outlooks.

Oates was sorely disappointed at the beasts that were his charge given, complaining that they were too old for the task and *"a wretched load of crocks"* to his eyes. In fact, it came to such a head that Oates very nearly gave up his position, and would have done but for the reason that the expedition was British, and that he took great pride in furthering his country to glory. In time, his views softened, and he admitted that perhaps the harsh conditions had further hardened his countenance.

As for the journey itself, the initial fifteen-strong crew set out from their base camp at Cape Evans on November 1st, 1911 on a typical blindingly bright, snow-laden day. The perilous cold would grow even more dangerous still, as the expedition journeyed the eight hundred and ninety-five treacherous miles towards the pole. The initial leg went as well as it could have gone, the snow and ice hard-packed, allowing the group to drive the horses across its surface. On January 14th, 1912, the first leg completed in a timely manner, the supporting members of the expedition were sent back to base by Scott. This left only five members, Oates among them, to hike that last one hundred and sixty-seven mile stretch to the pole.

Seventy-nine days after their departure, January 18th, 1912, the Terra Nova expedition found itself at the South Pole, only to discover a tent already standing brazenly against the harsh winds of the Antarctic. Inside, notes were discovered, detailing a competing Norwegian expedition's journey and their own success, only thirty-five days ago, on December 14th, 1911. The group, disheartened at this discovery, yet still gladdened to have accomplished a goal that only those five men could claim as well, allowed themselves a short respite before embarking on the return trip to Cape Evans.

The group immediately faced an excess of the tribulations of being in the Antarctic. Difficult conditions plagued them at every step, namely an horrifically adverse weather pattern, which contributed to terrible perception behind frost-crusted goggles, leading to several falls and stumbles into hidden ledges and crevasses. Poor food supplies led to a weakening strength, and several members fell victim to scurvy and frostbite. Oates was not immune to these ailments; on the contrary, he suffered greater than the average. His feet were severely frostbitten, blackened and corpse-like, and it is possible that his old war injury, that awful gunshot wound to the thigh, had reopened due to the effects of scurvy. In his diary, Scott wrote on March 5th, *"Oates' feet are in a wretched condition... The poor soldier is very nearly done."*

On February 17th, 1912, the Antarctic claimed its first victim, Edgar Evans, with the cause suspected to be a blow to the head sustained several days prior after a particularly nasty fall. Progress had been slow before then, but it grew more snail-like by the day. With an average of sixty-five miles between food and fuel deposits that were to last a week apiece, as there was nothing to scavenge for survival other than frozen water, the group needed to maintain a moderate pace of nine miles a day in order to have full rations for the final four hundred miles across the Ross Ice Shelf. Alas, nine miles was their best day ever, and as they pressed ever onwards, their march slowed, only making three miles a day at times due to Oates' worsening condition. The entire group suffered greatly, with extremities threatening to freeze and snap off without warning, and mouths filled with blood due to lesions that refused to heal. Oates was by far in the most wretched state of them all.

On March 15th, Oates reported to his comrades that though his spirit was still strong, his body was failing him beyond any resolute outlook, and asked the group to leave him in his sleeping bag, and continue without him. Though the rest of the team was suffering, they pleaded with Oates to continue with them, and were unwilling to leave the man to a certain icy death. Oates relented, and managed a few more miles, but could go no farther that day, and his situation deteriorated rapidly through the night.

On the morning of March 16th, Oates stalwartly set his boots aside and, looking to the men he had willingly marched with into an environment by its very nature inimical to man, stoically spoke to them. *"I am just going outside and may be some time."* Then, despite objections, he strode outwards into a blizzard, and the -40°C temperatures that accompanied it, to his self-imposed death. Scott wrote in his diary, *"We knew that poor Oates was walking to his death, but though we tried to dissuade him, we knew it was the act of a brave man and an English gentleman."*

Unfortunate to the highest degrees, this valiant act was likewise in vain, and made no difference in the eventual outcome. After this stirring sacrifice, the last three men forced themselves another twenty miles towards the 'One Ton' food depot that could have been their salvation. But, they were halted at latitude 79°40′S by the increasingly fierce blizzard on March 20th. Forced into seclusion in their tent, and too weak, cold and malnourished to continue, these brave men died nine days later, only eleven miles short of their objective. Their frozen bodies were left untouched for many months, until a search party discovered them on November 12th, 1912.

As for Oates, his body was never found. The search party, upon coming to where they believed it likely he had strode into the furious snows, erected a cairn and a cross, which to this day bears the following inscription:

Hereabouts died a very gallant gentleman, Captain L. E. G. Oates, of the Inniskilling Dragoons. In March 1912, returning from the Pole, he walked willingly to his death in a blizzard, to try and save his comrades, beset by hardships.

THE LAST ORDER OF FIRST LIEUTENANT JOHN R. FOX

$\mathcal{R}$ISING through oppression and adversity to accomplish grand acts is a scenario repeated time and again in the exemplified history of humanity. Mistreatment and abuse will not deter such people; nay, they draw upon an inner strength that defies what would otherwise bring out the worst traits, the forefront of which being egotism. One such man that defined an altruism few can contemplate, let alone enact, was First Lieutenant John R. Fox. Born in Cincinnati, Ohio in 1915, Fox was subjected to the systematic persecution endemic to all men of colour at the time. Despite these difficulties, he was hard working and studious, and attended Wilberforce University with an enrolment in their Reserve Officer Training Corps program, graduating with a commission of Second Lieutenant in 1940. During these trials, Fox had the principles of leadership ingrained into him permanently, among those being valour, determination, and, foremost, self-sacrifice, a trait which would in time be enacted without hesitation.

Fox was inducted into the 92nd Infantry Division at his graduation, a segregated section of the United States Army colloquially known as the Buffalo Soldiers. Upon the outbreak of World War II, Fox was sent to help slow the western advance of Axis forces, and eventually turn the tide. Fox spent years bravely honing his leadership skills and serving distinctively, with care not given for colour or creed. His valiant service earned him a promotion to First Lieutenant, and his skill led him to deadlier assignments that only a seasoned veteran could tackle.

During the first few weeks of December 1944, Fox, then 29 years of age, had been serving as a member of Cannon Company, 366th Infantry Regiment, 92nd Infantry Division, as a forward observer with the 598th Field Artillery Battalion - that is to say, Fox would scout enemy positions and relay coordinates via radio to artillery teams, allowing them pinpoint accuracy at great ranges. During this month, American forces had been forced to slowly withdraw from the village of Sommocolonia, in the Serchio River Valley of Italy, after overwhelming German forces initiated ferocious assaults to retake the town. By Christmas Day of 1944, only a token American force remained in the town, as the majority had made a tactical retreat to muster a stronger offensive. During that night,

Axis forces infiltrated the village, clothed in civilian garb to allay suspicions of enemy action. By early morning, the town was largely in hostile hands and the Germans commenced a strike by uniformed soldiers accompanied with heavy artillery bombardment at 0400 hours.

As American forces were greatly outnumbered, they had the difficult decisions of making an ultimately futile stand, or withdraw from the town under darkness and live to fight another day. However, Lieutenant Fox and a small number of his observer team volunteered to stay behind and do what they could to assuage the oncoming forces by calling in defensive artillery fire. By 0800 hours, Fox reported massive German infantry forces attacking in the streets in strength, and began to order shelling of particularly concentrated groupings and important choke points.

Nonetheless, despite a slowed advance, the Germans continued to make progress, causing Fox to adjust the artillery closer and closer to his own position. Eventually, Fox was warned that his given coordinates were too close to his own position, and he risked grievous bodily harm or even death should such an order be followed through. Fox repeated his desired shelling coordinates, and watched from the second story of his house as craters erupted from brick and dirt fountains from just outside his window. Machine gun fire hosed the wooden walls as dozens of German infantrymen swarmed not twenty yards away, with devilish intent to overrun the last holdout of the American forces that had maimed and killed hundreds of their compatriots.

Realising the necessity of his last order, Fox reported his own coordinates for artillery fire. The receiving officer, stunned at this, asked for a clarification, replying that this would bring deadly fire on top of his own position, surely a death wish. Fox simply replied *"Fire it."* He then hastily removed himself from his radio and took up his last stand at the top of the stairway, attempting to delay the advance by the precious seconds required for the shells to arc from their barrels and thunder into the home. Germans stormed the entryway and crashed through the windows in a ferocious assault, hoping to storm the house in a wave of flesh and metal. Fox fired endlessly from atop the staircase, heedless of both the death surging from below, and falling from above.

Death-dealing shells whistled through the air and utterly obliterated the structure, transforming it from a strong defensive position to a deadly shrapnel grenade of wooden splinters as long as a man's arm and cracked brick capable of denting skull. The house exploded instantly from the barrage, the concussive blast levelling it and the surrounding landscape into little more than a mixture of base components. Those that briefly heard that distinctive sound of shell coming had no choice but to face their mortality.

In time, a counter-offensive was launched and with great thanks to Fox and his expert, calculated observation, the town was retaken from the beleaguered German forces. Fox' last known position was uncovered - the house a blackened, useless shell, surrounded by bodies in great numbers. His supreme sacrifice allowed the delaying of enemy forces until other artillery and infantry units could repel the attack. Lieutenant Fox' body was found amongst approximately one hundred Nazi uniforms, an accurate count was difficult to compile given the devastation. His body recovered, he was shipped home and given a military burial, befitting his rank, status, and gallantry, and buried in Colebrook Cemetery in Whitman, Massachusetts.

At the time, Lieutenant Fox was awarded the Purple Heart, the Bronze Star and the Distinguished Service Cross for his courageous action. In the 1990s, it was found that black soldiers were unduly denied consideration for the Medal of Honor based solely on their race. After review, seven soldiers had their Medals upgraded on January 13th, 1997 by then President Bill Clinton; First Lieutenant Fox was among those seven. Posthumously, he was awarded the Medal of Honor and his surviving widow accepted it on his behalf over fifty years after his death.

After the war, the citizens of Sommocolonia erected a monument in honour of the nine men that died during the artillery bombardment. Of those men, eight were Italian soldiers, defending their homeland from the German forces. The last was First Lieutenant John R. Fox, who made the greatest sacrifice possible for the ideals he had sworn to uphold.

THE SINKING OF A
GERMAN U-BOAT DUE TO
AN IMPROPER FLUSH

$\mathcal{D}$URING the closing days of World War II, the faltering Third Reich continued its submarine operations off the coast of the British Isles. They pressed onwards, unwilling to admit defeat despite the overwhelming odds they now faced. U-boats, originally the most dangerous predators of the Atlantic Ocean, had begun to be weeded out by the encroaching advances in technology, but were still a fearsome threat. They stealthily stalked the underwater currents, listening intently for vessels ferrying men and supplies, easy targets from the hidden vantage point afforded by the deep, dark waters.

One specific member of the German fleet, designation *U-1206*, was on its first patrol off the coast of Peterhead, Scotland in mid-April of 1945. The commander of the U-boat, Kapitänleutnant Karl-Adolf Schlitt, was eager to display a show of success, as the boat had yet to have even a single confirmed hit on an enemy vessel, much less sink one. Brash and eager for a kill as he was, KptLt. Schlitt at times ignored standards of operation in favour of taking shortcuts for the sake of simplicity, or merely a belief that such minor points were beneath his perception; this prideful outlook would be the source of his greatest failure.

This particular ship was designed and built far later in the Third Reich's attempt at conquest, than the first iterations and in particular it possessed a very unusual and complicated toilet. It was a vast improvement on earlier models, allowing its usage at much higher pressures, and, as such, lower depths. Unfortunately, the toilet had a rather complicated procedure for its use, and, although not necessitating the mind of an engineer to use, it did necessitate a specific order of actions. On April 14th, 1945, *U-1206* was cruising at about two hundred feet beneath the surface, quietly scanning its surroundings, when KptLt. Schlitt decided to use the interlude to take a brief respite with the toilet. This proved to be the advent of disaster.

After completing his business, KptLt. Schlitt attempted to flush the toilet, but in his haste misunderstood the mechanisms for doing so, causing it to malfunction. Recognising his mistake, KptLt. Schlitt called for a specialist to report, in order to resolve the issue. After arriving on scene, the ill-trained crewman attempted to reroute the water supply through manipulating the appropriate valves, but in doing so accidentally caused massive amounts of seawater to enter the ship and strain the piping system, causing it to shut down immediately. With alarms blaring and gauges fluctuating wildly, the crew raced to their posts in a fevered attempt to stem the oncoming flow. But the damage was done, and the water flooded the lower levels, its corrosive nature invading every corridor and corner. With mounting panic, KptLt. Schlitt realised nothing could be done to prevent the seawater rushing into the batteries situated deep beneath the toilet.

As the ocean water collided with the batteries, it bubbled and frothed angrily, producing an incredibly poisonous chlorine gas, which dissipated rapidly throughout the vessel. Coughing, gagging, choking, the men scrambled away on shaky legs, their vision blurred and senses impaired. Knowing that there was no alternative at this point, KptLt. Schlitt ordered an immediate surfacing of the U-boat, risking being spotted instead of the sure fate of death that awaited them below the waves. Its hull popping and groaning with the sudden pressure changes, U-1206 quickly ascended the roughly two hundred feet to the surface, its breaching sending forth a burst of white foam and causing an outcry amongst the numerous sea birds lazily flying about the area.

The birds were not the only residents of the skies off the shore of Peterhead, Scotland. A Royal Air Force patrol happened to be flying above, on the lookout for the dastardly Krauts attempting to gain a toehold within their precious islands. Fortuitously, the ever-watchful eye of the RAF happened to spot U-1206 on its ascent, and, fearing an imminent assault, immediately reported back to the airfield with their findings. During these proceedings, the crew of the U-boat began to rapidly vent the noxious gas and filter in clean air, oblivious to the fact that their location had been noted with alarm, and indeed was soon to be assaulted by the RAF.

The gas cleared, KptLt. Schlitt made orders to repair the damaged valves, replace the worthless batteries, as well as clear the vessel of its remaining water. At this point, a low buzz was heard amongst the crew topside, as they retched over the side due to the effects of the gas. Searching the horizon, a squadron of aircraft were spotted flying in from the mainland, and KptLt. Schlitt was alerted of the advancing danger via the panicking crew. Notwithstanding the massive repairs needed, KptLt. Schlitt made orders to dive with astounding speed, preferring a possible escape and later repair instead of surely being destroyed now. Despite his alacrity, the U-boat could not respond with similar nimbleness, and only sluggishly attempted to manoeuvre. This delay was all the Royal Air Force required. A lightning-fast response enabled the performance of a bombing run upon the hampered vessel, completely disabling its engines and causing it to take in water with absurd speed, not to mention injuring scores of crewmen and killing four outright due to the high explosives.

KptLt. Schlitt was convinced of the futility of attempting to save his U-boat at this point, and gave the order to abandon ship. The crew took no time in complying, rapidly discharging themselves into the frigid waters, with KptLt. Schlitt following suit. The *U-1206* unceremoniously began to sink, eventually descending the seventy meters to the ocean floor with nary a complaint. With pained, disgruntled faces, their bulky life jackets causing them to bob like corks, the sailors started their pitiful swim to land. In the space of only an hour, KptLt. Schlitt went from being the commander of the *U-1206*, one of the most advanced and deadly weapons in the naval arsenal of the Third Reich, to a frozen castaway paddling to the Scottish mainland, known now almost exclusively as the man that sunk a U-boat all because he could not flush a toilet properly.

CHARLES DARWIN AND THE TAMING OF THE TORTOISE

$\mathcal{T}$HE year of 1831 was a pivotal time for the energetic, as-yet unproven Charles Darwin. After the conclusion of his final exams at Cambridge, he departed for a short geological survey in Wales for several weeks, after which time he was to return to Cambridge for theological training. However, the 22-year old student and inquirer of the Natural World was not meant for such a continuation, as fate intervened to alter the course of his life forever. Captain Robert Fitzroy, commander of the *HMS Beagle*, a warship of some ten cannons and no small amount of acclaim in the pursuit of scientific endeavours and exploration, was planning to depart from England, 'round the South American coastline and advance well into the spirited waters of the South Pacific. As his previous commander had lost his life by his own hand due to the extended isolation on a similar venture, Captain Fitzroy decided to take upon his crew a "gentleman passenger" of a sort, for good company and to record the observations of the voyage.

Inquiries were made to a number of professors amongst the elite of British academia, which in turn put Captain Fitzroy in touch with the recently unencumbered Darwin. So impressed was the captain with Darwin's wit in conversation, adherence to appropriate scientific endeavours and zest for adventure that it was a foregone conclusion that Darwin should be invited aboard the *Beagle* upon its departure. And so, in the year 1831, Darwin left England for five years, and in that time he would lay the foundations for what would become one of the most revitalising and influential theories of the Natural World.

Only two days after Christmas, 1831, the *Beagle* departed for the Canary Islands, then pressed onwards to South America, which was reached by February of 1832. Considerable exploration had been completed, both coastal and inland, by Darwin until partway through 1835. During this time Darwin, oftentimes alone, ventured forth into the dangerous wilds and observed terrible counts of slavery and barbarism amongst the native people. His steely demeanour and unopposable countenance preserved him and he remained unscathed despite the horrors of the lands he traversed.

In September 1835, Darwin and the crew of the *Beagle* reached the Galapagos Islands, whose mysteries delighted him to no end. Chief among those wonders was that of the giant tortoise, the sheer bulk of which amazed Darwin and crew alike. Upon sight of these lumbering beasts on the shoreline, Darwin's heart raced, so momentous was the occasion. He observed them at a distance for a short while, then, exercising a caution gained only from snatching one's life from the hands of death time and time again within the bounds of the South American continent, crept closer, the palpitations of his heart thundering in his ears. Within but a dozen yards away, a turtle spied Darwin's approach and appraised the, to it, strange and unencountered creature, determining friend, foe, or something else entirely. In hesitation, the great beast withdrew into its impervious casing, a shell of such prodigious girth and hardness that it, to Darwin's reckoning, easily would support a man. The spark of ingenuity and sheer daredevilry flared into existence within the recesses of his mind.

Darwin, with renewed confidence, strode up to the immobile tortoise and examined it intently, intensely curious about its make-up and potential origins. In a passion, he seized an opportunity that he thought may never again present itself and clambered up the craggy shell, firmly planting himself at its height with scarcely concealed glee. With a great deal of coaxing and sustained patience, the reptile once more extended its limbs and began to move about, either unaware or unconcerned with its newfound passenger. Such shock and amazement befell his fellows, in stark contrast! This man, both gentleman and scholar, striding out on these virgin beaches and with great aplomb placing himself most excitedly on the backs of these monstrous creatures. It was as if a child had taken hold of Darwin's mental faculties, and chosen this monumental occasion to make its presence known for posterity, with no concern as to the societal standing of poor Darwin once the moment had passed.

Upon later recollection in Darwin's journals, he wrote that the mounting and riding, exhilarating though it was, proved to be a difficulty over time. Darwin attempted this feat on several more occasions, with his balance improving upon repetition. Within those journals were found several schematics for a harness and saddle system perfectly suited to the unusual size and shape of the tortoise, as well as behavioural notes concerning their possible breeding and raising tame. Unfortunately, such plans have been lost to the ravages of time, but it is well within the realm of conjecture to postulate that, given further opportunities, we might now have had herds of trained Galapagos Tortoises at our call.

Annals of Honourable Persona

Xerxes I (519 BC-465 BC), Persia
John of Bohemia (1296-1346), Bohemia
Benjamin Hornigold (ca. 1680-1719), England
James Cook (1728-1779), England
John Kendrick (ca. 1740-1794), Massachusetts
Bhakti Thapa (1741-1815), Nepal
Jeanne-Geneviève Garnerin (1775-1847), France
Hugh Glass (1783-1833), Pennsylvania
Charles Robert Darwin (1809-1882), England
David Livingstone (1813-1873), Scotland
Lawrence Edward Grace Oates (1880-1912), England
Lorenz Peter Elfred Freuchen (1886-1957), Denmark
John Malcolm Thorpe Fleming Churchill (1906-1996), England
John Robert Fox (1915-1944), Ohio
Dashrath Manjhi (ca. 1934-2007), India
Arland Dean Williams Jr. (1935-1982), Illinois

29980136R00061

Printed in Great
Britain
by Amazon